Runes on

Fay Sampson lives in a Devon village. Her 26 novels, for both adults and children, include the Dark Age fantasy series, *Pangur Bán*, drawing inspiration from the poetry and art of Celtic monks, and two historical novels about the conversion of Anglo-Saxon kingdoms, *A Casket of Earth* and *The Flight of the Sparrow*. While researching the background to her fiction, she became fascinated by the history of the British Isles after the Romans left. The result was *Visions and Voyages* (Triangle), a history of the Celtic Church told through stories from the early sources. *Runes on the Cross* tells the companion story of the Anglo-Saxon Church.

To Annie

Runes on the Cross

*The Story of Our
Anglo-Saxon Heritage*

Fay Sampson

TRIANGLE

First published in Great Britain 2000
Triangle Books
Society for Promoting Christian Knowledge
Holy Trinity Church
Marylebone Road
London NW1 4DU

British Library Cataloguing-in-Publication Data

A catalogue record for this book is available from the British Library

ISBN 0-281-05268-9

Typeset by Pioneer Associates, Perthshire
Printed in Great Britain by
Caledonian International Ltd, Glasgow

Contents

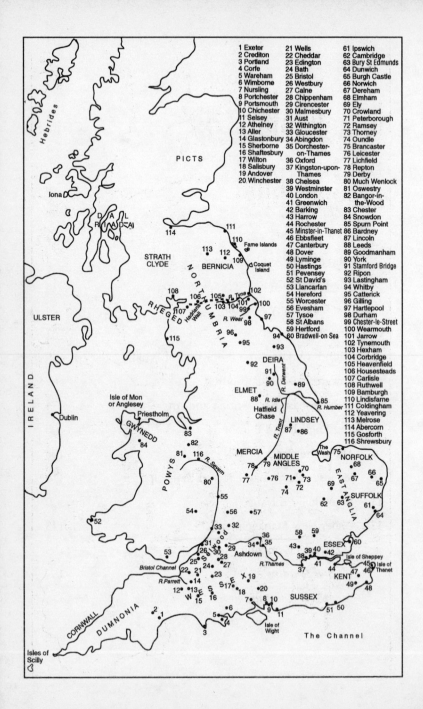

1 Exeter
2 Crediton
3 Portland
4 Corfe
5 Wareham
6 Wimborne
7 Nursling
8 Portchester
9 Portsmouth
10 Chichester
11 Selsey
12 Athelney
13 Aller
14 Glastonbury
15 Sherborne
16 Shaftesbury
17 Wilton
18 Salisbury
19 Andover
20 Winchester
21 Wells
22 Cheddar
23 Edington
24 Bath
25 Bristol
26 Westbury
27 Calne
28 Chippenham
29 Cirencester
30 Malmesbury
31 Aust
32 Withington
33 Gloucester
34 Abingdon
35 Dorchester-on-Thames
36 Oxford
37 Kingston-upon-Thames
38 Chelsea
39 Westminster
40 London
41 Greenwich
42 Barking
43 Harrow
44 Rochester
45 Minster-in-Thanet
46 Ebbsfleet
47 Canterbury
48 Dover
49 Lyminge
50 Hastings
51 Pevensey
52 St David's
53 Llancarfan
54 Hereford
55 Worcester
56 Evesham
57 Tysoe
58 St Albans
59 Hertford
60 Bradwell-on Sea
61 Ipswich
62 Cambridge
63 Bury St Edmunds
64 Dunwich
65 Burgh Castle
66 Norwich
67 Dereham
68 Elmham
69 Ely
70 Crowland
71 Peterborough
72 Ramsey
73 Thorney
74 Oundle
75 Brancaster
76 Leicester
77 Lichfield
78 Repton
79 Derby
80 Much Wenlock
81 Oswestry
82 Bangor-in-the-Wood
83 Chester
84 Snowdon
85 Spurn Point
86 Bardney
87 Lincoln
88 Leeds
89 Goodmanham
90 York
91 Stamford Bridge
92 Ripon
93 Lastingham
94 Whitby
95 Catterick
96 Gilling
97 Hartlepool
98 Durham
99 Chester-le-Street
100 Wearmouth
101 Jarrow
102 Tynemouth
103 Hexham
104 Corbridge
105 Heavenfield
106 Housesteads
107 Carlisle
108 Ruthwell
109 Bamburgh
110 Lindisfarne
111 Coldingham
112 Yeavering
113 Melrose
114 Abercorn
115 Gosforth
116 Shrewsbury

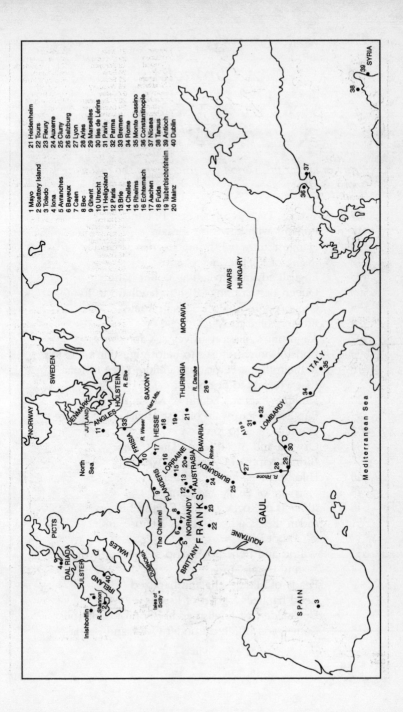

1 Mayo
2 Scattery Island
3 Toledo
4 Iona
5 Avranches
6 Bayeux
7 Caen
8 Bec
9 Ghent
10 Utrecht
11 Heligoland
12 Paris
13 Brie
14 Challes
15 Rheims
16 Echternach
17 Aachen
18 Fulda
19 Tauberbischofsheim
20 Mainz
21 Heidenheim
22 Tours
23 Fleury
24 Auxerre
25 Cluny
26 Salzburg
27 Lyon
28 Arles
29 Marseilles
30 Iles de Lérins
31 Pavia
32 Parma
33 Bremen
34 Rome
35 Monte Cassino
36 Constantinople
37 Nicaea
38 Tarsus
39 Antioch
40 Dublin

A Chronology

Many dates for this period are uncertain. The following is an approximate guide.

367	Saxons, Picts and Irish raid Britain
410	Romans withdraw from Britain
428	Hengest and English mercenaries arrive
442	Rising of English mercenaries
495	English advance halted at Mount Badon
560	Queen Bertha brings Bishop Liudhard to Kent
575	Gregory sees English boys in Rome
584	Edwin exiled to Wales
597	Augustine's mission arrives at Canterbury
603	British Church refuses to help Augustine's mission
616	Aethelfrith the Ferocious's children flee to Iona
	Essex reverts to heathenism
627	Paulinus baptizes Edwin of Northumbria
	Baptism of Earpwald of East Anglia
632	Paulinus flees to Kent
634	Oswald and Aidan found Lindisfarne
635	Birinus baptizes Cynegils of Wessex
640	Hild becomes nun at Hartlepool
643	Marriage of Oswy and Eanfled
644	Ithamar of Rochester first English bishop
651	Aidan dies. Cuthbert enters Melrose under Abbot Eata
653	Wilfrid and Benedict Biscop set out for Lyon and Rome
	Peada of Middle England baptized
	Cedd baptizes Sigbert of Essex
	Deusdedit first English archbishop of Canterbury
655	Conversion of Mercia under Oswy and Peada

Apology

No self-respecting novelist has characters with the same initial regularly appearing in the same scene. The scribe of history has no such freedom to use the 'Replace' key. The Anglo-Saxons, alas, had a policy of naming whole families with the same initial, even the whole first syllable. 'Aethel' means 'noble'. It was much favoured for boys and girls of – well – nobles. Readers are counselled to pay more attention than usual to the second half of the name. Think of Aethelbert as Aethel Bert. Where nicknames are known, I have added them to help. In Anglo-Saxon names 'ce' is pronounced 'ch'. Chad was originally Ceadda. Otherwise, 'c' is usually 'k'.

The Anglo-Saxons were an assortment of Germanic peoples. From early on, they called themselves collectively the 'English'. I have used 'Anglo-Saxon' and 'English' interchangeably. 'British' means the Celtic people who occupied most of Britain before they arrived. 'Picts' were an older people. 'Scots' were of Irish descent.

'Pagan' derives from the Latin word for 'country people'. In recent times there has been a move to reclaim it. A computer programmer from the home counties may nowadays confess it with pride. 'Heathen' is the Anglo-Saxon equivalent. It means 'those of the heath'. It seems appropriate to use it, as the Anglo-Saxons themselves did, for the pre-Christian religion of their people.

1

Who are the Anglo-Saxons?

Three immensely long rowing boats sweep in from the North Sea. Burning shoulders heave and the westering sun bleeds on the flashing oars. A harbour mouth opens. A stone fort guards it, but no one challenges them. The crowd on the quay has fallen still to watch. The faces turned to these ships are apprehensive, yet no one runs away. The strangers sense that they are expected, but hardly welcome.

From the beaked prow, the chief shouts an order. Big-built men and sturdy women slacken their stroke and the ship glides against the wharf. Children peer over the gunwale, wide-eyed with excitement, fretful with exhaustion. Their parents look about them, weary and wary. The houses cluster more closely here than they are used to. But there are rich meadows, cornfields. This, then, is Britain.

They start to clamber ashore, unloading cargo. The air is harsh with the protest of cattle lurching down the gang-plank, shrill pigs, the flapping of poultry in wicker coops. The wharf fills up with their blankets, chests, cooking pots, the precious things of home. They have come to stay.

A British boy, innocent that half his native island will one day be England, tugs at his father's hand with an urgent question. In a language they do not yet understand, he asks, 'Who are they?' But the answer his father makes is clear enough. 'Saxons.'

ORIGINS

The year is 460. The Romans have been gone from this island 50 years.

The people we call 'Anglo-Saxons' came from several Germanic tribes. The Jutes made landfall in Kent and the Isle of Wight from the Jutland peninsula or the banks of the Rhine.

Saxons came from the north German plain, between the rivers Weser and Elbe. They left their name in Essex, Sussex, Middlesex and Wessex. Angles set sail from Holstein, at the base of the Danish peninsula, and from its islands, steering for the coasts of East Anglia and north of the Humber. Others arrived from lands as far apart as Frisia in the Netherlands and Moravia.

To the British, they were indiscriminately 'Saxons'; the Scots still use the name 'Sassenach'. And this reflects reality. They were all from a large Germanic area, from the Rhine to the Danube, from the Alps to the North Sea, variations of a widespread culture. There might be minor differences of dress and jewellery: a Saxon woman fastening her tunic on each shoulder, a fashionable Jute in striped skirt and fitted jacket. They spoke different dialects of a common language, but neighbours could probably understand each other's speech, as modern Welsh- and Cornish-speakers do. For themselves, they soon adopted the inclusive name 'English'. In time, their separate territories became one 'England'.

They were part of a greater Indo-European culture, which had swept westward, its common origins fragmenting into a diversity of local languages, customs, art. The Celtic Britons and the Romans were themselves Indo-Europeans. We find shared words, artistic symbols and mythological stories, from India all the way to Ireland. The Sanskrit sky god 'Dyaus' became the German deity 'Tiuz'.

A WARRIOR CULTURE

The seafarers landed in a Britain which the Roman empire had abandoned 50 years before. Their Germanic homelands had never fallen to Rome. As they looked about them, they were startled by the legacy of imperial occupation. Stone fortifications seemed to them like the work of giants. Romano-British villas, with colonnaded courtyards and baths, were a thought-world away from their finest gabled timber halls. The very idea of cities was alien to them. They preferred to spread themselves widely over the countryside, four or five farmsteads to a hamlet.

But the Britons were drifting back to a life not so very different from the Anglo-Saxons'. Roman towns were abandoned to weeds and trees. The single province of Britannia was splitting into warring kingdoms. Without the legions along Hadrian's Wall, the British were prey to the Picts from the north. Roman coastal defences no longer guarded Britain from Saxon warships or Irish pirates.

For the Anglo-Saxons disembarking, Britain held out opportunity. The mid-fifth century had seen a rise in sea levels. Low-lying coasts of northern Europe were being lost to the encroaching waves. Others had left the severe winters of inland forests and bogs. Southern and eastern Britain offered a milder climate, fertile farmland. The food they wanted was simple: cattle, sheep, pigs, poultry and grain. They were great drinkers, brewing copious quantities of ale from barley.

Above all, Britain held out the promise of warfare, to protect her against raiders. Her rulers were promising food, land and treasure. The Anglo-Saxons' was a heroic culture: fighting was their highest virtue. Tacitus, a Roman writing in the first century, says that a Germanic bride and bridegroom exchanged gifts of weapons. The men scorned agriculture, leaving it to those too weak to fight. They lived on the generosity of their leader, demanding gold or spears. Their chief required, in return, their utter loyalty. Warriors presented him with treasure they had won, even ascribed their own heroic deeds to his name. A chief fought surrounded by his band of companions, who swore not to leave the battle alive if their leader fell. When this warlike people became Christians, they hailed Christ as their 'young hero', leader of his companions, dying gloriously.

The warrior's typical weapons were a spear and round shield. Few had breastplates and helmets were the prized possessions of the élite. To keep a warband in food and weapons, and to win renown, a chief needed battles and booty. If there was peace at home, he would seek war on someone else's territory. A fifth-century commentator from Gaul complained of the Saxons, 'They outdo everyone else in brutality. They're ungovernable and completely at home on the sea.' With the departure of the Roman war machine, Britain was a promising client for battle-hungry mercenaries in the protection business.

The Anglo-Saxons brought their Germanic gods. To our great regret, they did not write down their myths, which were celebrated only in song. It is the old problem with a non-literate culture: what we know comes from foreign observers, often their enemies, or passed into writing centuries later, heavily edited by Christian scholars. Another branch of this Germanic culture took root in Scandinavia. A rich store of Norse sagas has been preserved. But by the time it was committed to writing, some five centuries had separated Scandinavia from our Anglo-Saxons. Their myths had evolved, become more sophisticated. It is hard to disentangle what might once have been early common belief.

CREATION DEITIES

The echo of an earth goddess found its way into an early English charm.

> Erce, Erce, Erce,
> Mother of Earth . . .
> Hail to you, Earth, Mother of humans:
> Grow great in God's embrace.

This charm was still chanted in Christian times. Before ploughing, a loaf was baked, using every kind of flour, kneaded with milk and holy water, and laid under the first furrow.

Tacitus says the Angles worshipped an earth goddess, Nerthus, whose sanctuary was an island in the North Sea. Once a year, she emerged from her grove, veiled, to make a triumphal tour of the villages in her chariot. There was feasting and rejoicing wherever she went. No one dared break her peace. Then chariot, veils and goddess were taken down to a lake, to be washed by slaves and returned to her secret grove. The slaves were drowned in the lake.

Hilltops, sacred trees and wells were centres of worship. The Norse told how the world was sustained by a giant ash tree, whose roots reached down into the shadowy abodes of the dead and whose branches soared to the city of the sky gods. This tree was threatened by the Frost Giants, who would destroy the world. Germany had sacred oaks. Idols were carried out of the groves into battle. The most important sanctuaries had wooden temples to house the sacred images, probably wooden pillars, symbolically carved, rather than detailed human representations.

There is evidence of a sun goddess and a moon god. Some English people still turn over coins at the new moon, avoid seeing the new moon through glass, or sow their gardens by the lunar calendar.

The Anglo-Saxons believed in giants, tree people, light and dark elves who captured witnesses to their moonlit dance, dwarves underground and monsters in pools, kobolds who would do your chores for a saucer of milk. Goblins lurked, ready to attack you in the darkness of the forest or the desolation of the fen. The countryside was alive with the numinous and dangerous.

Besides these elemental beings, whose presence was felt in every waking activity, there were families of gods with power over human life. Every week, we honour four Anglo-Saxon deities who were major players in the mythical drama.

TIW

Tuesday is dedicated to Tiw. The French name, *mardi*, reminds us that the Romans linked him with Mars. Tiw's name comes from the same root as Zeus and an even older Indian Sky-Father. In time, he was ousted from the supreme position and became another warrior god. Tysoe overlooks the Vale of the Red Horse. Such a horse may be his warlike symbol, cut in the hillside.

WODEN

Wednesday is the day of Woden who usurped Tiw's pre-eminence. To the Germans he is Wotan, in Scandinavia Odin. The French call his day *mercredi*, because the Romans equated him with Mercury, who led the souls of the dead to the underworld. Woden is linked with Wode 'the Mad', the Fury who rides at the head of the Wild Hunt on stormy nights, leading the spirits of the dead. There are reports of human sacrifices to him on hilltops.

The Norse told how Odin thirsted to drink from the well of wisdom at the foot of the World Tree. The demon who guarded the water demanded one of Odin's eyes. He paid it willingly for wisdom.

Another myth brings us closer to the crucified Christ's own story. Odin hanged himself on the World Tree, wounded by his own spear, sacrificing himself to himself. For nine days he hung, without food or drink, until he saw beneath him the runes of sacred knowledge. With a stupendous effort he stooped and snatched them up. The power of the runes set him free; he rose rejuvenated, the wisest of all gods. We cannot be sure that the same story was told of the English Woden, but poems about the cross as a tree and the power of runes make it probable.

Runes were straight-sided signs, both letters and symbols. They were cut as brief inscriptions. Tacitus tells how in Germany they were written or carved on slips of fruit wood and flung on to a white cloth. The priest, or the father of a family, prayed, then picked them up. The pattern they formed determined the future. To be able to write runes was a mark of magic.

Wisdom has the power to heal. In the Nine Herbs Charm, 'The serpent came creeping; it tore a man in pieces. Then Woden took nine glorious twigs and struck the viper so that it flew into nine parts.' In a German poem, Woden heals the foot of the young god Balder's foal, knitting the wrenched bones together. The English repeated this charm over their own livestock in the Christian era, replacing Woden's name with Christ's.

In the heroic Anglo-Saxon culture, wise Woden had to become a war god. But he was not a weapon-wielder. He directed battles from the sky. The Scandinavian Odin became the host of Valhalla, welcoming slain heroes to his glittering feasting hall. It is doubtful whether the Anglo-Saxons ever believed in Valhalla.

Woden's name is found more widely across England than any other god's. His awesome power is evident in the name Wansdyke, which the English gave to a great earthwork meandering across 60 miles of the chalk hills of Wiltshire. Elsewhere there are Grimsdykes, and the prehistoric flint mines named 'Grimes Graves'. Grim, the 'Masked', is the name under which Woden visits the human world disguised. At a gallows at the crossroads, an immensely tall, cloaked figure stares knowingly at the victim hanging there. Two ravens on his shoulders croak intelligence. He swivels his low-brimmed hat. From the shadow of his bearded face his one eye pierces you. Woden, as Grim, is the forerunner of countless wizards of fantasy.

Woden was a god for aristocrats. Most Anglo-Saxon royal families traced their genealogy back to Woden, even after they were converted to Christianity. The exception is Essex, whose kings claimed as their tribal ancestor the god Saxnote, about whom we know nothing.

WALKYRIES

Wagner's operas have popularized a stirring vision of Valkyries, helmeted maidens swooping over the battlefield, carrying off the bravest warriors whom Odin, or Wotan, has chosen for Valhalla. There is no evidence that this concept ever held sway over English imagination. There are certainly Walkyries, but they are more primitive. The Anglo-Saxons saw them as pursuing creatures of nightmare. Woden's Wild Hunt sweeps the stormy night accompanied by a pack of black hounds with hideous glaring eyes. Even as women, they are terrifying.

Loud they were . . . when they rode over the gravemound,
Fierce they were, when they rode over the land . . .
The mighty women betrayed their power,
yelling as they hurled their spears.

THUNOR

If Woden is the god for aristocrats, Thunor is a rollicking, hot-tempered god for the common people, the farmers. He was Donnar to the Germans, Thor to the Norse. Goats drew his chariot across the storm clouds and he hurled his thunderbolt across the mountain peaks. With that thunder come showers of life-giving rain. Thursday is his day. To the French, it is *jeudi*, the day of thundering Jove or Jupiter.

Thunor is a gigantic, red-bearded figure, armed with an axe or hammer. He can be a friend, protecting against humans and giants and fertilizing the fields. If he loses his temper, he can blast a tree with one blow of his weapon. Trees, especially oaks, are sacred to him. He is a mighty trencherman. In the Scandinavian stories his gargantuan thirst lowered the level of the sea. Only death, who wrestled with him in the form of an old woman, was strong enough to overcome him.

He sailed into the deep ocean and let down a bull's head as bait to catch the World Serpent who engirdles the earth. Just as the cosmic struggle between the two was about to begin his terrified boatman severed the line.

Some, at least, of these stories were told in England. We find an illustration, carved on a Christian cross at Gosforth in Cumbria, of Thunor letting down the bull's head on his fishing line.

FRIG

Friday celebrates Frig, the 'Beloved', daughter of Earth and mother of gods. Something of her nature is suggested by the French name *vendredi*, the day of Venus, goddess of beauty and love. Yet romance hardly features in Anglo-Saxon poetry. Its predominant virtue is stoicism. What mattered was that a woman should bear children. Frig is a fertility goddess.

There is tantalizing evidence of other goddesses. Boxing Night, the start of the Anglo-Saxon year, was the 'Night of the Mothers'. In 'Solmonath', or February, cakes were presented, probably to the sun. The months we know as March and April were dedicated to the goddesses Hretha and Eostre, from whom the feast of Christ's resurrection was named Easter. We assume they were goddesses of spring growth. October was the 'Month of Offerings', presumably a harvest festival. November was 'Blood Month'. Animals were culled then to conserve feed through the winter and it became an occasion for ritual sacrifice.

WAYLAND SMITH

The Franks Casket is a walrus ivory box, its lid and sides ornamented with scenes from ancient stories. An inscription in runes tells where the ivory came from:

> the fish-flood lifted the whale's bone on to the rocky coast; the ocean was in turmoil where he swam aground on the shingle.

The rest is a fascinating mixture. On one panel the three Magi bring gifts to the Christ Child. Side by side with this scene sits the wise smith Wayland. Behind his deformed leg lies a body. The smith is holding its severed head with a pair of tongs. He extends his other hand towards two women.

Most mythologies have a smith. He is often feared by other gods for his secret craft and he suspects them of exploitation. Fragments of English poetry suggest a Norse story.

King Nidhad's soldiers stole a marvellous gold ring from Wayland's smithy. Wayland fell asleep dreaming his swan-maiden lover had come back to claim it. He woke in fetters. King Nidhad accused him of stealing his gold and gave the ring to his daughter Beadohild. The queen, fearing Wayland, ordered his hamstrings to be cut and had him marooned on an island, making jewellery. Two small princes crossed secretly to this island. Wayland cut off their heads and hid the bodies in a dunghill. He presented the unsuspecting Nidhad with their skulls mounted in silver and the queen with their jewelled eyes. Beadohild had breast ornaments carved from her brothers' teeth. Intrigued, she broke Wayland's ring and made this an excuse to visit him without her father's knowledge. He plied her with beer and raped her. Revenge complete, he soared away on magic wings he had made.

Precious gifts fascinated the Anglo-Saxons. What is interesting about the Franks Casket is that the Christian gift scene is

11

helpfully labelled 'MAGI'; the gift of the heathen Wayland Smith appears to need no explanation.

BALDER

In a Scandinavian story, Balder, the beloved, was the youthful favourite of all but the troublemaker Loki. His mother Frig exacted a promise from every living thing not to harm him. Only the mistletoe was deemed too young to swear the oath. The other gods amused themselves hurling every manner of weapon at Balder, confident that nothing could hurt him. Then Loki discovered the secret of his vulnerability. He fashioned a spear of mistletoe wood and gave it to the blind god Hoder. That cast killed Balder and the whole earth mourned him. Grief for a beloved young god dying from a spear wound echoes through the early Christian English poem 'The Dream of the Rood', as it vividly describes Christ's passion.

WYRD

Woven deep into the English language is the memory of Wyrd. It means 'to become'. Wyrd is destiny. Even the gods are subject to her. Scandinavian myth has three Norns. They weave the destiny of the universe on a huge loom, made from the first branch cut from the World Tree. Their number in England is uncertain. But allusion to 'Wyrd' and 'loom' and 'web' are there in plenty. Resignation to a fate already woven haunts the earliest English poems. A later Christian poem says,

> Great are Christ's powers;
> Wyrd is strongest.

Centuries later, Shakespeare's witches know Macbeth's destiny, hailing him by his present and future titles. He calls them 'the weird sisters'. This powerful sense of Wyrd was reconciled within Christianity as God's will.

Priests served these gods. A priest of Woden was forbidden to carry weapons or ride a stallion. Yet holy men and women conducted their own warfare, chanting spells from high ground to bind the enemy's hands. Women were believed to have special gifts of holiness and prophecy. Men consulted them and took their advice. Kings and chiefs had sacred duties on which the welfare of their people depended.

This was the religious baggage the Anglo-Saxons brought to Britain. It was not a comfortable faith. In life, the jolly fertility god Thunor could at any moment blast your crops. One night, Woden's ghastly troop might snatch you up, if Wyrd had woven your life's end. A symbolic ship might carry the rich out into the grey chill over the horizon. A shadowy underworld awaited the rest. Yet stoically, stubbornly, the Anglo-Saxons who landed in Britain fought and gave birth and honoured their gods.

2
The English Conquest

MERCENARIES

The British monk Gildas looked back on those Anglo-Saxon landings with horror. Around 540, he wrote *The Ruin of Britain*. He fulminates against the 'proud tyrant' who invited the 'unspeakable Saxons' into his land to butcher or enslave his people. This is not the whole truth. There had been Anglo-Saxons in Britain for centuries.

The 'Roman' army was recruited from all over the Empire and even further afield. Some came from Germania, that great swathe of middle Europe. Frontline fighting was often done by foreign troops under their own officers. Germanic warbands volunteered. Their boorish behaviour made them unpopular with the locals. 'Notfried's troop' left their name carved at Housesteads fort on Hadrian's Wall. Some may have married Christian Britons.

But increasingly Saxons came as raiders. The Roman 'Count of the Saxon Shore' coordinated defences against them. A chain of forts guarded the east and southern coasts, from Brancaster, near the Wash, to Portchester. There are Saxons buried in cemeteries beside these forts. The Romans had persuaded some to turn from poacher to gamekeeper. Burgh Castle in Suffolk was commanded by a Saxon. Saxons had a reputation as fine sailors, as well as fighters. They probably served in the Roman coastal patrols, using blue sails and blue uniforms for camouflage.

RAIDERS

The High King of Ireland married a Saxon queen in the fourth century. In 367 he coordinated a terrible raid of Irish, Picts and

Saxons on different parts of Britain. The Irish fell on the west, the Picts on the north; the Saxons went for the south-east. Some Saxon garrison troops mutinied to join them. Killed on the defending side was a general with a Germanic name, Fullofaudes.

A writer from Aquitaine says the Saxons were in the habit of dedicating one tenth of their prisoners to Woden by hanging or drowning. But they were swift raids, for booty. In the fifth century the Saxons began to eye Britain as a promising land for settlement.

Saxons and Picts struck again in 429, after the Romans left. Germanus, bishop of Auxerre and a former army general, was visiting Britain. He went to assist the Britons. The Saxon warband advanced into a valley between rocky walls. Suddenly the stillness was shattered by echoing yells, 'Alleluia!' It seemed as though the sky and the hills were falling in on them. They fled back across the river, leaving many drowned.

But one defeat did not deter them. Soon they were back, by invitation.

HENGEST

Vortigern was a British king with a power base around Gloucester. His name is really a title: 'Overking'. He decided to follow Roman practice and hire Germanic mercenaries to protect Christian Britain against raiders. He was able to get other British kingdoms to agree to his plan and grant his Jutish mercenaries land in Thanet, then separated from the rest of Kent by a wide channel. The British agreed to pay them food and weapons.

Tradition says the mercenaries were led by the brothers Hengest and Horsa. In an early Anglo-Saxon poem, Hengest is the leader of a Danish fighting band, who accompanies his king Hnaef on a visit to Finn Focwalding, king of Frisia. Fighting breaks out and the Danish king is killed. Hengest and his men fight the Frisians to a standstill and then enlist in Finn's service. Next year, Hengest kills Finn and becomes leader of his Jutish warband.

A few hundred mercenaries landed at Ebbsfleet on Thanet.

When the scale of the danger facing Britain was apparent, Hengest proposed sending for more. English settlements began to appear beyond Kent, in East Anglia and Essex, along the Lincolnshire coast and west as far as Portsmouth. Saxons and Picts renewed their attacks. More mercenaries went to Hadrian's Wall. Hengest suggested attacking the Irish, but this offer was not taken up. There were no early English settlements in western Britain.

With peace, the British leaders grew restless. They told the English, 'We don't need you now. There are so many of you, we can't keep on feeding you and giving you weapons. Go home.' It was a false economy. The British were in no position to eject unpaid mercenaries. Just when the British needed to be most united, they fell apart in civil war. Vortigern appealed to the English for help. More ships arrived. Tradition says that one of them brought Hengest's daughter, and that Vortigern got very drunk and proposed to her. As bride-price, he promised Hengest the whole kingdom of Kent. Unfortunately, he failed to tell its British king he had given his land to the English.

And still they kept coming. The original island homes of the Angles were said to have been left uninhabited.

In 442 the English lost patience. They demanded the payment they had been promised. When it was not forthcoming, they rose against the British. Gildas writes of his country swept by fire. Roman towns fall to the battering rams. People, priests and bishops are mown down as weapons flash and flames roar. The streets are purpled winepresses, strewn with dismembered bodies. The British can only find burial under ruins or in the bellies of beasts and birds.

Understatement is not Gildas's style. The English were still a minority. The carnage did happen, but not everywhere, even in the south and east. Hengest did not take London.

The British leaders asked for a truce. Vortigern and the leading councillors of the British were to meet the English around the table, both sides unarmed and seated alternately. Suddenly, at a shout from Hengest, the English pulled from their boots the *seax*, the long knife from which the Saxons get their name. Three hundred British leaders were slaughtered. Only Vortigern was spared, and forced to grant still more land.

A symbolic story of this struggle is told about a fortress Vortigern tried to build on Snowdon. Each day the workmen assembled timber and stones. Each night they disappeared. Vortigern's seers advised him to sprinkle the foundations with the blood of a child who had no father. A boy was found, whose mother said she was a virgin. This wise child insisted on a better solution. He advised digging. Under the foundations they discovered a pool, and in that pool two vessels and a cloth. When the cloth was unwrapped, it disclosed two sleeping dragons: the British red and the white dragon of the English. The dragons fought. For a time, the white dragon seemed to be winning. But finally the red dragon drove it off the cloth and into the lake. That boy is known to us as Merlin.

The white dragon of the English advanced ever further west. Britons who survived slaughter fled to the forests, mountains and cliffs, or were enslaved. Many sailed off to Brittany. We do not know how many stayed to serve or intermarry with the English. The English language replaced the British in the south and east.

With each acre gained, Britain became a more secure and inviting place for English settlers. By the late fifth century, ships were filled with families as often as with warriors. They were farmers, avoiding the cities. St Albans, London and York remained British for a long time.

ARTHUR

Then the red dragon turned. British horsemen, with scarlet plumes and swords, were pitted against the ash spears of Saxon infantry. Cavalry without stirrups could strike fast, but not hit hard. The English shield wall often held.

Towards the end of the fifth century emerged the shadowy figure we know as Arthur. His conclusive victory over the English was Mount Badon, possibly near Bath. The English found themselves held behind a line approximately along the Fosse Way and the river Trent. For 50 years their western advance was halted.

Legend says that Arthur fell fighting his treacherous son Medraut and that Angles from Suffolk fought on Medraut's side.

The English were feeling the pressure now. Their ploughing methods restricted them to light alluvial soil. They did not yet work the heavier clays or clear the forests. Some of the English took ship too. Many accepted the invitation of Frisian kings and settled across the Channel in underoccupied land of the Low Countries.

ENGLISH KINGS

These early English settlers came in small bands from their continental homelands. They did not bring their kings. It was said of them that 'every oarsman is a pirate chief; they all share in ruling and obeying'. Many individual warleaders, with their kin and companions, occupied territory and killed, drove out or subjugated its British population. The more powerful consolidated their position and became recognized as kings of a wide region.

Aelle and his South Saxons landed in the mid-fifth century and massacred the British at Pevensey. Few Celtic place names survive in Sussex. It was the last English kingdom to accept Christianity. Their leader Aelle was the first to be given the name of *bretwalda*, a somewhat exaggerated title meaning 'ruler of Britain'. He had no authority over the surviving British kingdoms in the west, and the English north of the Humber went their own way. But other southern English leaders acknowledged him as overlord. Like all English kingship, the title was not hereditary. It had to be earned.

Cerdic came ashore at Southampton Water to claim the land of the West Saxons, Wessex. He is one of several West Saxon kings whose names have a British origin. It suggests early intermarriage here.

Essex, land of East Saxons, included London. It took over Middlesex. Mercia was the land of the 'border folk', up against the British around the Trent. Lindsey and the Isle of Wight were at first independent English kingdoms. There was even a separate territory of Hastings.

From early on, the Angles north of the Humber stood out from the rest. They were separated from the south by the British kingdom of Elmet, around Leeds. Ida was the first to be recognized as king of Bernicia, north of the Tyne. His queen had a British-sounding name. Around 550 he seized the black basalt crag of Bamburgh, overlooking the Farne Islands. To the south was Deira, an English kingdom around York.

These pioneer leaders were not rulers in the countries they came from. The Angles in the east seem to have had a more highly developed sense of kingship. The first king to move his whole court from the homeland was Icel. He founded a royal centre for his North Folk in East Anglia. The North Folk themselves were subdued by the South Folk when Uffa set up his court at Ipswich.

All over English territory, a society in which there had been few distinctions was becoming more aristocratic. Men were previously buried with spear and shield, women with simple jewellery. Now distinctions become apparent. Some men are buried with swords. Women of distinction have more elaborate goods, perhaps a crystal ball hung from the girdle, or an iron weaving sword which packed the threads on her loom. Until the late sixth century, no horse gear was buried in Anglo-Saxon graves. One writer jested that the English did not even know what a horse looked like. Now, we find the warleader riding to battle while the rest march.

Germanic kings were originally chosen from among a group of chieftains, to lead the army. 'King' meant 'son of the kindred'; 'queen' meant 'woman' or 'wife'. Kings were invested with a helmet rather than a crown. It was a temporary appointment, not needed in peace. In these frontier conditions of Britain the army needed to be on a regular war footing. Kingship became permanent. But it was still a role to be earned, not inherited by primogeniture. The best leader was chosen from among the royal kin. The king's role was to win glory in battle and to give his followers rich gifts; the duty of his warriors was to give him their loyalty and their lives, and to render treasure back to him out of the riches they won. When the English hailed Christ as their King, this is the active heroic model they held in their imagination. Centuries later, the golden crown of Christ enthroned on the cross was called his 'helm'.

As the Saxons pressed west, an urgent plea went to the abbey of Llancarfan in Glamorgan to pray for the British troops and curse the Saxons. Finnian, an Irish monk, answered the call. He tried persuasion first. The Irish were more generously-minded towards the invaders than the British Church. It was not their country which was being devastated and conquered. Finnian went to the English camp, in a valley between high hills, and counselled them to go home in peace. Only when they refused did he lead the British around the heights over-looking the valley. He had his pilgrim staff in his hand and he showed them how he meant to deploy it. Rocks crashed down on the English, inexperienced in this mountainous terrain.

The Christian British reacted with horror to the English advance across their island. They were filled with loathing at the refugees' stories of murder, rape and enslavement. They could not entertain the idea of converting their conquerors. Their only thought was to exterminate them or flee. Even when the hated English became Christians, they would not sit down to eat with them and insisted any dish they used must be scoured before it was fit to eat from again.

But the Irish had other ideas. Late in the fifth century, Aben, an Irish monk, founded a monastery on a hill above the Thames at Abingdon, in territory recently overrun by Saxons. In the late sixth century, the Irish Columba had two English monks in his monastery on Iona. There were unrecorded Saxon conversions.

BERTHA

Profound change began in Kent. This south-eastern kingdom had always been subject to Frankish influence. The Frankish kingdoms of Gaul and beyond were ruled by the powerful Merovingian family. They were Christians, though that did not prevent them from engaging in bloody family feuds.

Bertha was the daughter of the Frankish Christian king of Paris. Around 560, she married Aethelbert, English king of Kent. He would have been small beer to Bertha's Merovingian connections, but he was an ambitious young warleader, who was soon hailed by the other kings as *bretwalda*.

Bertha came from a family of strong-minded women. Her forebear Basina came to her great-grandfather, king Childeric, declaring her intention to marry him. When Childeric asked why she wanted to desert her first husband for him, Basina replied, 'If I knew of a more capable and energetic warleader across the Channel, you can be sure I'd have picked him instead of you.' This Germanic tradition of women of authority and initiative was soon evident in the first English abbesses.

Bertha agreed to be Aethelbert's bride with conditions. She and her retinue must be free to practise their Christian religion. She brought her Frankish bishop, Liudhard, as chaplain. This expatriate community discovered that the Kentish capital of Canterbury had known Christians before them. Its imperial grandeur had fallen into decay, the wooden English buildings sprouting among crumbling stonework. But there were churches still visible. Bertha and Liudhard took over St Martin's, outside the walls.

There is no record that they attempted to convert others. This may seem surprising in the light of later transformations of English kingdoms, which happened when Christian princesses arrived as brides with their chaplains. Irish missionaries to Europe at this time condemned the Frankish Church as decadent and unwilling to evangelize. Bertha's eldest son does not appear to have been baptized. There was none of the concern for mission which became an outstanding contribution to Europe from the Anglo-Saxons themselves. But it is probably to Bertha's presence that we owe what happened next.

GREGORY'S PLAN

'Angles or angels?' That joke changed the history of England.

Gregory was an aristocratic politician and a Benedictine monk. He was walking through the market place in Rome when his attention was caught by a group of boys being offered for sale. He was struck by the exotic beauty of their blond hair, fair-skinned faces and finely-cut features.

He was told they were Angles. Jesting that, with faces like

that, they looked as if they ought to be sharing eternity with the angels, he questioned more closely. Where exactly did they come from? 'Deira', north of the Humber. Gregory punned on that too. *De ira* is Latin for 'from wrath'. These Angles must be saved from judgement by Christ's mercy. Who was their king? 'Aelle'. Gregory's mind leaped to 'Alleluia!'

He knew that heathens were conquering Christian Britain. This stark fact was now transformed into human beings. He saw in front of him, not the hosts of evil, but English boys, far from home, bewildered, scared, defiant. He was filled with desire to go and bring these lost sheep into the Christian fold.

It was a bold vision. Christians often penetrated foreign lands, taking the gospel with them, with profound consequences. But they rarely set out with the intention of converting an entire nation. Gregory's concern may not have been only for the Anglo-Saxons' salvation. The capital of empire had shifted to Constantinople. Barbarians had swept southwards, attacking the very gates of Rome. Eastern churches looked to Constantinople, Antioch, Jerusalem, Alexandria. Western churches operated with increasing independence. Irish scholar-monks were spreading Celtic Christianity abroad. If Gregory could bring Britain under the influence of Rome again, it would be a significant boost for Rome's authority.

He even set out. But Gregory was a trusted figure in dangerous times. The Roman citizens staged a demonstration to have him called back. He was acclaimed pope. Twenty years passed before his dream could be realized and he was not the missionary. And the mission did not come to the Angles north of the Humber, but to Kent, with its Christian queen.

AUGUSTINE'S MISSION

To lead his mission to the English, Gregory chose the prior of St Andrew's, a Benedictine abbey in his own house in Rome. This Augustine, a native of Marseilles, is not to be confused with the great fifth-century Carthaginian who wrote *The City of God* celebrating the grace of God, and also gave us the notion that original sin is a sexually transmitted disease.

Augustine set out for Britain in 596, accompanied by an

unusually large force of some 40 monks. In southern Gaul their courage failed. How could they survive among heathen savages, whose language they did not speak? They sent Augustine back to explain this impossibility to the pope. Gregory would have none of it. The harder the labour, the greater would be their eternal reward. He promoted Augustine to the rank of abbot and sent him off with letters of recommendation to bishops and rulers along the way. Early in 597 they landed on the shores of Kent, bringing Frankish interpreters.

King Aethelbert viewed these alien priests with suspicion. He ordered them to be held in quarantine on the isle of Thanet. There Thunor's Mound was sacred to the thunder god. Aethelbert came to meet the newcomers, but he insisted that it be in the open air, under the canopy of his sky god. He did not want to be trapped by the magic of another God within the confining walls of a building.

Augustine's band made a brave show of hiding their own fears. What the king saw coming was a procession, led by monks carrying a silver cross and a wooden board painted with Christ's image, singing a Latin litany for salvation – their own as well. Aethelbert listened while Augustine preached. He was impressed with the Christians' sincerity and their Lord's promises, but not yet converted.

Still, he offered the Romans lodging in Canterbury, a food supply and permission to preach to his Kentish people. The monks entered the city in a chanting procession, behind their cross and banner.

At first, they joined Queen Bertha's congregation at St Martin's. The little church began to make English converts. Augustine and his companions lived an austere and simple life in Canterbury as a religious community. Their missionary duties did not permit them the full observance of a monastery, but they maintained a discipline of prayer and fasting.

King Aethelbert was persuaded to accept Christ. He did not compel his subjects to follow him, but his baptism released a flood of converts. Gregory wrote jubilantly to the patriarch of Alexandria that 10,000 Anglo-Saxons were baptized on that first Christmas Day. The English Church had begun.

3
The Canterbury Mission

THE KENTISH CHURCH

Kent's new Church needed a bishop. In the Roman Church, the diocesan was the key figure. There is a curious silence about Bertha's chaplain, Bishop Liudhard. Perhaps he was already dead. Roman episcopal consecration was performed by at least three bishops, to ensure the validity of apostolic succession. There were British bishops in the unconquered west of the island, but it was not to them that Augustine appealed for consecration. He had heard that the British Church was no longer fully in the Roman tradition. To ensure his episcopy was above question, Augustine went back to the archbishop of Arles.

But how should this infant Anglo-Saxon Church proceed? Augustine sent Gregory a letter asking a string of questions. It was 601 before Gregory, concerned with the defence of Rome and so ill that he could only work a few hours a day, sent answers. They are models of moderation, with not a little exasperation at Augustine's anxieties.

No, of course women were not made unclean by childbirth or menstruation, and could attend church. Yes, he could baptize expectant mothers. But the Anglo-Saxon custom of a man marrying his widowed stepmother could not be permitted.

Augustine should respect the authority of the archbishops in Gaul, but offer criticism in a brotherly spirit. He should stop worrying about the different practices he had seen, just select the best for his English Church and bind them into one sheaf. With the British Church it was different. Gregory gave Augustine authority over its bishops, but he did not communicate this fact to them.

Of course, Augustine could consecrate a second bishop on

his own. How often did he expect to get a visit from Gaulish bishops? Once there were more bishops for the English, the problem would solve itself.

Gregory had a vision for the English Church. He sent Augustine the *pallium*, a lambswool stole which was his elevation to the rank of archbishop. He planned another 12 bishops, initially under Canterbury, but with the metropolitan see moving to London after Augustine's time. If the mission proved successful in the north, there should be a second archbishop for York, also with 12 bishops under him. After Augustine's death, seniority would move between York and London, residing with the archbishop consecrated first.

Gregory's plan had far-reaching implications. He envisaged the English kingdoms, indeed the whole of Britain, as a single country, with two provinces, drawing his model from the days when Rome had governed all Britannia, at least as far as Hadrian's Wall. The present reality was a patchwork of rival kingdoms. The dream of the overall authority of the Roman Church generated a unifying vision for a future England.

Gregory envisaged a secular church in Kent, not one staffed by monks. The minor clergy, such as door-keeper or exorcist, should be allowed to marry, but not deacons or priests. Married clergy would live outside Augustine's celibate male community and would therefore need a stipend.

A thief who stole from a church should be judged with charity if the sin was motivated by poverty.

Augustine had boasted about the miracles he performed. In a private letter, Gregory counselled him against the sin of pride.

Gregory sent ecclesiastical vestments, liturgical vessels, holy relics for the new altars, and many books. He also sent reinforcements, including Justus, Mellitus and Paulinus, who became notable players in the English Church.

A letter to King Aethelbert urged him to destroy the shrines of idols. After the party set out, Gregory had second thoughts. He sent a messenger hurrying after them, with another letter. The barbarians needed to climb the mountain of faith step by step. It was not, after all, a good idea to destroy Anglo-Saxon temples, only their idols. Well-constructed buildings should be cleansed with holy water and fresh altars dedicated to the only God. The English could come to worship in familiar surroundings and enjoy their traditional festivals. Animals would not, of course, be sacrificed to the gods.

The epitaph inscribed on Gregory's tomb records that he 'led the Angles to Christ'.

EXPANSION

Aethelbert let the Romans restore an ancient church inside the walls of Canterbury. Christ Church became the first English – as distinct from British – cathedral. He also gave land east of the walls, and here Augustine founded the monastery of St Peter and St Paul.

The second see was Rochester, where Augustine made Justus bishop in 604.

The first foothold outside Kent was Essex. The conversion of King Sabert was helped by the fact that Aethelbert was both his uncle and his overlord. It was Aethelbert who built the wooden church of St Paul's in London, then a trading port within Essex. Mellitus was installed as its first bishop, with his cathedral looking across at the great pagan temple at Harrow-on-the-Hill.

AUGUSTINE AND THE BRITISH CHURCH

In 603 Augustine travelled across Britain to the lower Severn near Aust. Across the mudflats rose the mountains of the unconquered Celtic lands. He called representatives of the British Church to meet him at a spot named afterwards 'Augustine's Oak'. Here he urged them to change their ecclesiastical practices, which differed from those of Rome, and to join with him in his mission to evangelize the English.

Neither side understood the other's thinking. The archbishop of Canterbury saw himself as representing the authority of the pope and the majesty of the English *bretwalda*. The leaders of the British Church believed themselves to be inheritors of ancient Christian tradition, dating back to at least the third century. They did not realize how things had changed on the continent or how far their own practices had adapted to Celtic society. With the collapse of cities and the rise of rural monasteries, abbots had become more important than bishops, ruling the Church like spiritual chieftains from their strongholds. Most seriously, these Britons had lost half their island to the English. Their people had suffered slaughter, rape, exile, enslavement. They could not bring themselves to offer the love of Christ to those who were even now threatening their last surviving lands. They asked for time to consult their people.

Abbot Dinoot of Bangor-in-the-Wood in North Wales led a throng of British Church leaders and scholars to the second meeting. Before they set out, they sought guidance from a hermit. Celtic Christianity placed greater value on communication between God and the individual. This hermit advised them to observe Augustine's body language. If he rose to greet them as equals, they could do business with him. As the British approached, the archbishop stayed in his chair, visibly asserting authority over them.

Insulted, the British accused him of arrogance and denied his demands. Augustine narrowed these down to three. They must conform to the Roman date for Easter, bring their baptismal rite into line with Rome's, and join him in carrying the gospel to the English. They refused. Their stubbornness appalled Augustine. The salvation of the Anglo-Saxons was the sole reason he had come to Britain. He cursed the leaders of the British Church. If they refused peace with fellow Christians, they should have war with their enemies. If they would not offer eternal life to the English, then they must suffer death at English hands.

Augustine himself died soon after. Wanting to avoid the lengthy delay in consulting Rome, he had appointed Laurentius to be his successor, a practice forbidden in the Roman Church. Laurentius met with no cooperation from the British either.

AETHELFRITH THE FEROCIOUS

North of the Humber another drama was being played out. In 588 Aethelfrith of Bernicia, known as 'the Ferocious', assassinated

Aelle of Deira, whose name had caused Gregory to cry 'Alleluia'. The kingdoms became one Northumbria. Aethelfrith's first wife had been a British princess, whose name, Bebba, means 'beautiful traitor'. Aethelfrith now took as his queen the assassinated Aelle's daughter, Acha. He set out to exterminate her male relatives.

Her nephew Hereric fled to the little British kingdom of Elmet, around Leeds. The heathen English prince and his wife Breguswith found shelter in a Christian court. But Aethelfrith's long arm reached even here. Legend says that Breguswith had a dream in which her husband was snatched away and she searched for him in vain. Then, under her skirts, she discovered a jewel, whose brilliance lit up all Britain. Hereric was poisoned. But Breguswith's daughter Hild became one of the great jewels of the Anglo-Saxon Church.

EDWIN IN WALES

That left only one male descendent of Aelle. Acha's four-year-old brother Edwin was also whisked away to a Christian British kingdom. He was fostered by Cadfan on the Isle of Mon, or Anglesey. Cadfan was a devout Christian, 'the most learned of kings'. He brought Edwin up with his own son, Cadwallon.

Anglo-Saxon tradition is silent about this part of his life. But Welsh sources say that Edwin was baptized by Rhun, a British warrior prince turned priest. At a Christian court, dependent on the protection of a Christian king and his God, Edwin might well have chosen to be baptized.

Around 616, Aethelfrith the Ferocious turned his wrath on Wales. King Cadfan rode out to meet him with other Welsh warhosts. Their armies met near Chester. Nearby lay the huge teaching abbey of Bangor-in-the-Wood, led by abbot Dinoot. The monks knew their duty. Having fasted for three days, hundreds of them assembled at the battlefield, to pray for the safety of Christian Britain and curse the English invaders. Aethelfrith saw them. He was, in his own fashion, as religious a man as the Christians. He feared the power of holy men as much as the spears of Welsh warriors. He decided to eliminate them. The English charged. The monks were massacred.

Edwin fled from Christian Wales to the heathen English kingdom of Mercia. He married its princess, who bore him two sons. Here he apparently reverted to the gods of his ancestors.

Still on the run from Aethelfrith the Ferocious, he moved to East Anglia. Its king, Redwald, had visited Kent and been persuaded by King Aethelbert to accept Christianity. But when he arrived home he was unable to convince his strong-minded queen and his councillors to endorse his decision. Redwald apostatized. But Edwin must have been startled to enter the temple of the Anglo-Saxon gods and find, among their blood-stained shrines, an altar dedicated to 'the White Christ'.

Aethelfrith offered Redwald bribes to hand Edwin over or assassinate him. Redwald refused. The bribes got bigger. Threats followed. One night, a friend came running to Edwin as he was preparing for bed and told him he must flee for his life. Redwald had given in and agreed to sell his life. The friend offered to smuggle him out to a secret hiding place. Edwin replied wearily that there was nowhere left to run. Resigned to his Wyrd, he said that, since death was inevitable, it would be better from Redwald's hand than from someone less noble. He sat on a stone outside his lodging, alone in the darkness.

A stranger approached. He asked Edwin why he sat alone, out of doors, in the middle of the night. Edwin retorted that it was none of his business. Unperturbed, the stranger asked what Edwin would give in return for his life, the restoration of his father's kingdom and more, and a future life and salvation unknown to his ancestors. Edwin promised loyalty to whatever power could bring that about. The stranger laid his right hand on Edwin's head and bade him remember his oath next time he felt this sign. Then he vanished into the dark. The friend came rushing back with the news that everything had changed. Redwald's redoubtable wife would not hear of him betraying the East Anglians' honour by giving up his friend for gold. Instead, they were raising a warhost. They would attack Aethelfrith the Ferocious and win Northumbria back for Edwin.

Two English warhosts met by the River Idle, south of the Humber. Redwald and Edwin won the day. Edwin entered

York as king both of his father's land of Deira and of Bernicia. He was, to all appearances, a heathen English king sworn to the worship of the Anglo-Saxon gods.

IONA

It was the turn of Aethelfrith's children to flee. He had one son, Eanfrith, by his British wife, and six sons and a daughter by Acha, Edwin's sister. They too found sanctuary in a Celtic Christian land. It was Iona, the island abbey Columba had founded in the Scottish kingdom of Dalriada. The daughter, Aebbe, was probably brought up by nuns on the Isle of Women. This image of Celtic monastic life made a lasting impression on these English children. They accepted Christianity. Aebbe received a proposal of marriage from Dalriada's king, Domnall Brecc, or 'Freckled Donald', but turned it down.

REVERSALS IN THE SOUTH-EAST

The young English Church depended on royal patronage. When Aethelbert of Kent died in 616, the Roman mission threatened to fall apart. His eldest son Eadbald turned the Kentish court back to heathen worship. Following Anglo-Saxon custom he married his widowed stepmother, in defiance of church law. Early Christian commentators blame his fits of madness on this.

The pattern was repeated in Essex on King Sabert's death. His three heathen sons entered St Paul's and demanded of Bishop Mellitus, 'Give us that white bread you fed our father with.' When he refused them the eucharist, they reacted with fury. He was offering it to common people, wasn't he? They drove him and his congregation out of Essex. He and Justus lost hope for the immediate future and fled to Gaul.

At Canterbury, Laurentius was on the point of following them. On the last night, he took his bed into the abbey church. After long and anguished prayer he fell asleep. In his extremity, he experienced a visit from the apostle Peter, who scourged him roundly for deserting his post. What sort of a shepherd was he who abandoned his flock to the wolves? Had he forgotten how Peter himself was beaten, imprisoned and crucified for Christ?

Next morning, Laurentius recounted this story to the king. It was a powerful performance. He stripped off his tunic and displayed the wounds. When Eadbald learned that he was the cause of the good man's suffering, he was converted to Christ.

King Eadbald repudiated his unlawful wife. He married a Frankish Christian princess and became a respected benefactor of Christian churches. But he remained tolerant of heathen religion. The idols stayed. In Kent, Justus was welcomed back to Rochester, but Mellitus never recovered the see of London. The worship of the Anglo-Saxon gods had a stronger hold in Essex than in any other English kingdom, if we can judge by place names.

Instead, Mellitus became the next archbishop of Canterbury. When Canterbury was on fire, he hurried to the church at the heart of the blaze, despite his gout, and commanded the flames to desist. He was followed as archbishop by Justus, then Honorius, both Roman missionaries. Augustine's church was holding on, but it was nearly half a century from the landing on Thanet before the Kentish Church had leaders with English names.

THE CONVERSION OF NORTHUMBRIA

Edwin of Northumbria became *bretwalda*. It was said that at the height of his power, a woman with a newborn baby in her arms could walk from coast to coast without being molested. Edwin's reach extended beyond the coast. He invaded the Isle of Mon, where Cadfan had given him shelter as a child. Cadfan's son Cadwallon was now king. Edwin hounded his foster-brother across his island home to a last refuge on the little isle of Priestholm. From there, Cadwallon fled into exile. Edwin renamed Mon, Anglesey.

He drove out the king of Elmet, the British kingdom which had failed to protect Hereric from poisoning. He incorporated it into Northumbria. Edwin's return must have been greeted with delight by Hereric's widow. Breguswith and her two small daughters, Hild and Hereswith, became part of the Northumbrian court.

In 625 Edwin, now widowed, took a second wife. It was a political marriage. Aethelberg, affectionately known as Tata, or 'Darling', was sister to the Kentish king. Like her mother Bertha, she came to her heathen husband with conditions. She must be free to practise her Christian faith and would bring her chaplain. Paulinus was consecrated a bishop to accompany her. Edwin agreed to take instruction in Christianity, with a view to conversion if his council consented. Tata also brought James the Deacon, a noted choirmaster.

On her first Easter Day in Northumbria, the court was at the royal villa on the Derwent. Tata was pregnant. An ambassador from a West Saxon king was announced. As he approached the king's seat, he whipped out a knife. Edwin's own loyal thane, Lilla, flung himself between his lord and the blade. The blow struck with such force that it not only killed Lilla but pierced the king he was shielding. There was a bloody struggle before the West Saxon met his end.

Tata went into labour. Edwin's wound was not deep, but the knife was poisoned and he was struck down with fever. That night, three lives hung in the balance: king, queen and unborn child. But Tata gave birth to a healthy daughter with little pain. Edwin recovered health. Paulinus hailed a triple miracle: three lives saved at the resurrection feast of the saviour Christ. He urged Edwin to accept baptism in gratitude.

Edwin prevaricated. He offered his daughter Eanfled as the first English Northumbrian to be baptized. But he would wait until Paulinus's God gave him vengeance on Wessex. At her baptism that Pentecost, little Eanfled took with her an escort of 12 Northumbrian converts.

The Northumbrian warhost marched south. Five West Saxon chieftains fell. But still Edwin would not commit himself. Pope Boniface wrote letters, urging the love of God. Edwin had given up visiting the temple. He no longer made the sacrifices traditional for an Anglo-Saxon king. He spent long hours in solitude, in deep anxiety. It was no light matter for a king to take from his people the protection of their ancestral gods. But an earlier baptism in Wales, of which his Christian queen and her bishop were unaware, may have weighed on his conscience. Could he confess to them that he, the great *bretwalda*, was an apostate, an oath-breaker?

Paulinus may unknowingly have offered a way out. He may have told of Augustine cursing the British Church for refusing to share Canterbury's mission. One of his three irreducible conditions had been reform of the Celtic baptismal rite. Was Edwin's baptism by Rhun valid?

One day, Edwin sat alone, deeply troubled. Someone approached. He felt a hand on his head. 'Do you remember this sign?' Edwin fell to his knees. Paulinus challenged him to keep the promise made in his extremity at Redwald's court. The bishop may have heard this story, but it is possible that he himself was the stranger who appeared to Edwin in East Anglia. Perhaps he had come from Kent, to urge Redwald to honour his baptismal promises.

Edwin called his council, the witan, and put the choice to them. Should they let Paulinus preach conversion to them? The account is startling. First to respond was Coifi, Deira's chief priest. 'I've served our English gods all my life, and what good have they done for me? You give gifts and honours to other people and ignore me. You haven't been near the temple for months, and still you win wars and the crops don't fail. I'm a laughing stock. If Paulinus's God can do better than that, I vote for change.' Another councillor drew their imagination to a sparrow, flying into the firelit hall out of the storm. 'For a few moments it finds warmth and shelter. Then it darts out at the opposite end and is lost in hail and darkness. Human life is like that. If Christ can offer us hope of more beyond death than chilly twilight, it must be better.'

Paulinus entered the hall. He was a charismatic preacher. The whole court rose to his call and committed themselves to Christ. Coifi the priest threw off his regalia. He demanded weapons and a stallion, forbidden to him while he was a priest of Woden. Armed with sword and spear, and riding the king's own horse, he led a frenzied raid on his own temple at Goodmanham. When the crowd saw him coming, they thought he had gone mad. Coifi flung his spear into the sanctuary, ritually defiling it. Then he ordered his troop to set fire to it.

Flinging a spear over the enemy in the name of Woden was a traditional Germanic way of declaring war. Coifi, in the name of Christ, was declaring war on heathenism. It was far from the moderate advice of Gregory to reconsecrate heathen temples for Christian worship. This was a warrior interpretation of Christianity.

THE CHURCH ADVANCES

A little wooden church was hastily built in York and dedicated to St Peter. On Easter Eve 627, the king was baptized with his family and court. His great-niece Hild was almost certainly among them. As in Kent, thousands loyally followed, their numbers daily swelled by Paulinus's preaching. At Catterick, Paulinus and James baptized thousands in the River Swale. They moved north to Bernicia. For 36 days they were at royal Yeavering, instructing converts and baptizing them in the River Glen.

Edwin's palace at Yeavering had huge wooden halls, glittering with gold. It also had a temple, which was apparently converted to Christian use. Holes once housed huge wooden pillars, almost certainly effigies of the World Tree and the Anglo-Saxon gods. They were uprooted and destroyed.

Paulinus came into Lindsey, south of the Humber, where Edwin had authority as overlord. One of those baptized by him in the Trent described the bishop as an awe-inspiring presence, tall, stooped, with black hair and a thin hooked nose dominating an ascetic face. The reeve, or governor, of Lincoln was converted and a stone church built. It was in this church that Paulinus consecrated Honorius archbishop of Canterbury.

Under Edwin's influence, the new king Earpwald of East Anglia, Redwald's son, accepted the Christianity his father had forsaken.

A SHORTAGE OF CLERGY

It reads like a huge success story. But the consecration of Honorius in Lincoln suggests something else. Paulinus may have been the only other bishop in the English kingdoms. The see of Rochester was vacant for a while, after its bishop drowned off the coast of Italy. Gregory's large band of Roman missionaries were dead or ageing. They had not as yet trained English leaders to succeed them. Earpwald of East Anglia was soon assassinated by an adherent of the old faith. His country lapsed back into heathenism.

Northumbria, too, saw the edge of shadow. Paulinus and Edwin were on their way back to the palace after a teaching session for new converts. A crow flew over, croaking ominously. Crows were sacred to Woden and watched for divination. The crowd eyed the bird, recalling their heathen past. Seeing the danger, Paulinus ordered a boy from his household to shoot it. The arrow brought the crow tumbling to earth. Paulinus joked that a bird that could not foretell its own death was hardly a trustworthy guide.

Such a vast flood of new Christians needed more than one priest. Accounts of the conversion of Northumbria, written only a century later, mention just two ecclesiastics: Bishop Paulinus and James the Deacon. James was a man of great energy, but he was not qualified to administer the eucharist. The diaconate was often undertaken as a lifelong career, with its own responsibilities. James's passion was church music and liturgy. It would seem obvious for Canterbury to send reinforcements, but we have no information that this happened. Kent was still recovering from its own setback.

Training English recruits was a long process. Men were not usually ordained to the priesthood before the age of 30. There is no hint that Paulinus founded a school or monastery in Northumbria. The impression we have is of a mass movement, largely the work of one man, without the pastoral support needed to maintain it.

Paulinus started to replace the wooden oratory of St Peter with a large square stone basilica, in the continental style. He did not stay to see it finished.

Nevertheless, Gregory's dream of two English Church provinces, based on London and York, was nearly realized. In 632 Pope Honorius despatched the *pallium* which would make Paulinus the first archbishop of York. Because of the difficulty of communication he sent another *pallium* to Canterbury, to be ready for whichever archbishopric needed it next. Communication was indeed slow. Twenty months before he wrote this letter, Edwin was dead and the Northumbrian mission had collapsed.

OVERTHROW

Penda was a warlord who seized control of Mercia. He made this hitherto insignificant midlands kingdom into one of the most feared war machines of the seventh century. He was an energetic defender of the old Anglo-Saxon religion.

He found an unlikely ally in Cadwallon, Christian king of Gwynedd. Edwin's foster-brother had returned from exile nursing a lifelong hatred of Northumbrians. Christian Britons and heathen Mercians met Edwin's warhost at Hatfield Chase, south of the Humber, not far from where he had defeated Aethelfrith the Ferocious. Here Edwin met the same fate.

Tata took her small daughter Eanfled and her baby son and fled by ship to her childhood home in Kent. Here she founded one of the first English monasteries for women, Lyminge. Paulinus lingered only long enough to collect up the church plate, including the great gold cross and chalice from St Peter's, and went with them.

James the Deacon stayed with his Northumbrian flock. When he could, he still preached and baptized. He lived in a village near Catterick, praying for happier days when he would once again be able to teach his beloved Gregorian plainsong. But James was not a priest. Without episcopal leadership, the six-year-old Church fell apart. The Anglo-Saxons expected their Lord to lead them to victory. The mass conversions turned back to heathenism as quickly as they had been won. There were pockets of the faithful, holding on. But only James's loyalty is remembered by history.

The Anglo-Saxon Church was back almost where it began. Kent was the only Christian English kingdom.

4
Lindisfarne

OSWALD BRIGHT-ARM

With the death of Edwin and the flight of Paulinus, the kingdom of Northumbria and its infant Church collapsed. Penda retired to Mercia, leaving Cadwallon to sweep through the territory with fire and sword. It was now the turn of the English to lament how Christian Britons put men, women and children to horrible deaths.

Northumbria was split again. In Deira, the new leader was Osric, a cousin of Edwin baptized by Paulinus. In Bernicia, the way was open for Aethelfrith the Ferocious's eldest son to return. Eanfrith was older than the other boys when they fled from Edwin. The Celtic Christianity of Iona had not made the same deep impression on him. Now he and Osric, with most of Deira and Bernicia, reverted to heathenism.

It lasted a year, a year so terrible the eighth-century historian Bede calls it the *annus horribilis* and decreed their reign should be expunged from the history books. Osric made an ill-judged attempt to besiege Cadwallon's base camp. He and his troops were slaughtered. Eanfrith attempted to negotiate. With 12 companions, he was admitted to Cadwallon's camp. If he believed respect for his British mother would save him, he was mistaken. He and his bodyguard were put to death.

News of this calamity reached Scottish Dalriada. Oswald Bright-Arm was the first son of Aethelfrith the Ferocious's marriage to Edwin's sister. He appealed to his protector, 'Freckled' King Domnall Brecc. Domnall loaned him a Scottish warband, with the proviso that they should not fight against Britons. In 633, Oswald Bright-Arm and his brother Oswy marched south. Very likely, monks of Iona strode with them as chaplains. As they entered Bernicia, survivors of the beaten Northumbrian warhost rallied to their standard.

They found their enemy by Hadrian's Wall, near Hexham. Oswald spent most of that night in prayer. He was strengthened by a brilliant vision of Columba of Iona, giving him the same encouragement Joshua had heard before he crossed the Jordan into the Promised Land: 'Be strong and courageous. See, I am giving you this land.' To the Church of Iona, Columba was second only to Christ. Very early next morning the Dalriadan warriors rose to this news. Oswald ordered his soldiers to dig a hole. With his own hands he held a rough-hewn wooden cross, while the men shovelled in earth to hold it firm. Before daybreak, he gave the order to charge. The Scots ignored Domnall's orders and attacked the British. Though greatly outnumbered, the northern force swept the field. Penda suffered his first major defeat. Cadwallon was caught fleeing beside a hillside beck and his throat cut.

The battle site was called Heavenfield. Bloody though it was, it changed not only Northumbrian political history but the nature of early Anglo-Saxon spirituality. Oswald's victory secured him the kingship of the whole of Northumbria. As a devout Christian, one of his first acts was to ask Iona for a pastor to guide the Northumbrian Church.

The first man chosen was Corman. He may have been with them as an army chaplain. Corman was a stern prophet. He found himself ministering to Bernician warriors who had only had fleeting contact with Paulinus. Most of those baptized had lost their faith under the trauma of defeat. Corman judged the Northumbrians barbarians, incorrigible in their obstinacy and sin, and returned to Iona in disgust.

Aidan and Lindisfarne

The man Iona sent to replace him was of a very different character. Aidan was an Irishman, a scholar, with an abbey of his own on Scattery Island at the mouth of the Shannon. Hearing Corman fulminate against the Northumbrian English, he recommended giving them the milk of the gospel first, before weaning them on to tougher meat. The monks of Iona voted him the best man for the task and he was consecrated bishop to the Northumbrians.

Aidan did not speak the English language. The difference between King Edwin and the new King Oswald was immediately evident. Edwin had loved status and ceremonial, having his standard paraded before him wherever he went. Oswald Bright-Arm, deeply imbued with the simpler spirituality of Iona, himself acted as Aidan's interpreter when he preached to the troops and the Bernician people.

Aidan and Oswald shared a love for the tradition of Celtic Christianity with its island monasteries, like Iona. They determined to create a holy island for Northumbria. Not far to the north of the royal fortress of Bamburgh lies the sandy outlier of Lindisfarne, to which it is possible to walk on foot at low tide. It was a very different headquarters from St Peter's in the Roman grandeur of York. It symbolized the Celtic relationship between church and court: close enough for frequent contact, but preserving a distance that gave it spiritual independence.

Here Aidan established a monastery and Iona sent monks to work there. Lindisfarne was not primarily for the contemplative life. The monks went out across the countryside, carrying their faith to the people. Most of our information about Aidan comes from Bede, who was loyal to the Roman cause and condemned the unorthodox Celtic churches. Yet the portrait he paints shines out as a marked contrast to Paulinus. He stresses Aidan's humility, not his impressiveness, and the deep love he inspired in everyone who met him. Aidan soon learned the English language and travelled right across Northumbria, visiting his flock. Whenever possible, he went on foot, so that he could talk to everyone he met. His monks were welcomed in the same way. People ran out of the villages to greet them. There are no records of great sermons and mass baptisms. The monks of Lindisfarne converted people by their example as much as by their words. This was the paradox at the heart of Celtic monasticism. Christians entered monasteries or became hermits to leave behind the sinful world, but love for the God they encountered there impelled them to serve him in this world.

They lived simply on Lindisfarne. They built a wooden

church, with a roof of reeds, which leaked. Grateful people gave them gifts, but the monks immediately gave these away to the poor. Or they bartered them to redeem slaves, many of whom used their newfound freedom to join the monastic community. When Oswald Bright-Arm visited Lindisfarne for spiritual guidance, he took only a small escort and was careful to leave before the monks' main meal, so as not to strain their meagre resources. If bad weather closed the way across the sands and forced to him to stay on, he shared the same simple food as the monks. When Aidan in turn visited the court, he ate only sparingly and retired early.

Oswald followed his soul-friend's example as well as an English warrior king could. He spent much time in prayer, before dawn, sitting with his hands palm upwards on his knees. He was generous, not only to his soldiers, as was expected, but to the poor. He had a servant to inform him of his people's needs. One day, Aidan came to supper at the court. They were raising their hands to bless the food when the servant came in to announce that there was a crowd of poor people begging at the gate. Oswald had the rich food from his table sent out to them, and ordered the great silver dish on which it had been served to be broken up and given away too.

Aidan had a deep love of scholarship. Anyone who travelled with him was expected to read the scriptures or learn the psalms as they went along. One of the first things he did was to set up a school on Lindisfarne to train English monks and priests for the future. There were 12 boy students in the school's first intake. Four of these were brothers: Cedd, Caelin, Cynibil and Chad. Another was Eata. These English boys grew up to play a significant part in the story of the Anglo-Saxon Church.

THE EAST ANGLIAN CHURCH

A similar shift happened in East Anglia. After the murder of Earpwald, Redwald's son, the East Anglians had relapsed into leaderless heathenism for three years.

The new king who emerged was Earpwald's half-brother Sigbert, who had fled to Gaul to escape Redwald's hostility. There he attended a monastic school and was baptized. He sent now to his Christian friends for help. The bishop who came was Felix, a Burgundian who had put himself at the disposal of the Canterbury church for missionary work. Sigbert gave him Dunwich for his see. Felix, like Aidan, saw the importance of a school to train English priests and recruited teachers from Canterbury.

Into this kingdom arrived another holy man whose style was very different from the Burgundian Felix. The vision of Celtic pilgrimage was a one-way journey, following the lead of the Holy Spirit. Fursey was an Irish monk who sought to escape the crowds who flocked to him. With a few companions, he set out on pilgrimage 'for love of the Lord'. Sigbert received him warmly. Fursey fell ill and in his fever experienced a vision commanding him to build a monastery. When he heard that, the king helped him set up a community in the ruins of a Roman fort, probably Burgh Castle in Suffolk. As with Aidan, Fursey attracted many to Christianity, not so much by his preaching as by the simplicity and holiness of his life. Those East Anglians already baptized were drawn closer to Christ by knowing him.

Fursey became famous for his visions, usually brought on by illness. He experienced angels carrying him through the skies, while evil spirits struggled to hold him back. Looking down, he saw the fires of falsehood, covetousness, discord and cruelty, and was burned on his shoulder and jaw by contact with a condemned sinner whose clothes he had inherited. Ever afterwards, people would find him sitting in a thin tunic on a bitter winter's day, yet sweating profusely at the memory of his terror and salvation. This hermit experience of a visionary struggle with evil runs from the founding Egyptian tradition of St Anthony, through the Celtic, on into the English Church.

Sigbert, inspired by this example, abandoned his kingship to enter the monastery he had founded at Bury St Edmunds. In 635, Penda of Mercia turned his warhost on East Anglia. The army commanders begged Sigbert to come out of retirement and raise the morale of the soldiers he had led in the past. When he refused, they dragged him out. But Sigbert still would not arm himself with anything more than his monk's staff. He was killed and the army defeated.

Bishop Felix's sound organization and Fursey's spiritual inspiration ensured that the East Anglians did not fall away from Christianity this time. Sigbert was succeeded by the devout King Anna, many of whose daughters and granddaughters chose the monastic life and became famous as abbesses or nuns. But the attacks of the Mercians eventually drove Fursey on to Gaul, still seeking the peaceful retreat for which he had left Ireland. He left his monastery to his brother Foilan and his hermit friends, to consolidate the conversion of East Anglia.

THE CONVERSION OF WESSEX

King Oswald's younger brother Oswy married the grand-daughter of Rhun, the British priest who had baptized Edwin. But Oswald Bright-Arm went to Wessex for his bride.

Christianity had newly come to the West Saxons. Bishop Birinus was possibly of Germanic stock. He was sent to Britain from Gaul under a direct mandate from Pope Honorius. He thus acted independently, bypassing the authority of Canterbury. He landed on the south coast, with a large vision for converting the midlands. But he was so distressed by the heathenism he found among these West Saxons that he realized he need go no further to find his mission field.

Birinus succeeded in converting King Cynegils, father of the sub-king who had tried to assassinate Edwin. He was aided by the fact that Oswald Bright-Arm was now Cynegils' overlord and a Christian. In 635 Oswald stood as baptismal sponsor to the West Saxon king. He then married Cynegils' daughter. The two kings gave Birinus Dorchester-on-Thames, near Oxford, as his see.

To Birinus, Cynegils and Oswald, as to Sigbert, Felix and Fursey, the difference between Roman and Celtic traditions was evidently less important than it was to Augustine's mission.

In 642, Oswald Bright-Arm led a campaign which drove Penda into Wales. Returning victorious, he had disbanded most of his army when Penda retaliated and attacked him at Oswestry. The Northumbrian king fell with a cleft skull. His last words were for his loyal companions dying around him: 'God have mercy on their souls.' Penda dismembered Oswald's body and exhibited his head and arms on stakes.

Next year, his brother Oswy led a daring raid into Mercia and retrieved Oswald's remains. The head was buried reverently in the church at Bamburgh and the arms interred on Lindisfarne. When one was exhumed it was found to be undecayed, fair-skinned and shining. Oswald was known thereafter as 'Bright-Arm'. He was on the way to becoming one of the earliest English saints, hailed for the Anglo-Saxon virtues of generosity in life and heroism in death.

Oswald Bright-Arm left a son, but he was not old enough to lead the warhost. English kings were chosen for their suitability, not merely their heredity. Kingship passed to his brother Oswy. But Mercia was back in power. It was a bitter blow to Oswy that he could not inherit the united Northumbria his father and brother had ruled. Penda gave Deira to Oswy's cousin Oswin, son of the apostate who had briefly ruled it in the *annus horribilis* after Edwin's death. Oswin of Deira was a Christian, a peaceable man, who submitted to Penda as his overlord.

The disaster which overtook the Northumbrian Church at Edwin's death did not repeat itself. Aidan did not flee and nor did the royal family. The Church of Lindisfarne proved deep-rooted enough to withstand the shock of defeat. Aidan continued to move across the boundary between Bernicia and Deira, as bishop to all the Northumbrians.

CRISIS IN WESSEX

The conversion of Wessex, however, hung in the balance. King Cynegils died a year after Oswald Bright-Arm. He was succeeded by his son Cenwalh, who had not accepted

Christianity. Cenwalh made the serious mistake of marrying Penda's sister and then repudiating her. Penda's wrath descended on Wessex. He drove Cenwalh into exile. But the West Saxon king found sanctuary in East Anglia, where King Anna was devoted to the Christian faith. When Cenwalh returned to Wessex three years later, it was as a Christian king.

OSWY AND EANFLED

The marriages of English kings had a profound effect on the English Church. When his British wife died, Oswy turned to Kent for his second queen. To strengthen his claim on Deira he married the exiled daughter of Edwin and Tata. As a baby, Eanfled had been the first Northumbrian Paulinus baptized. She was still a child when she fled to Kent. Her widowed mother founded an early English monastery for women at Lyminge.

There was a symmetry of reversed images in this marriage. Oswy's roots were in Bernicia, Eanfled's in Deira. He grew up in exile on Iona, she was an exile in Canterbury. He was steeped in Celtic Christianity, she loyally Roman.

Oswy sent Utta, his chaplain, to escort her on the North Sea voyage. Eanfled, as usual with royal brides, brought her own priest. Utta and the Italian Romanus must have eyed each other with suspicion. Utta was English, but he had his head shorn in the Celtic way, the front of the skull bare, with hair growing long behind, a tonsure probably adapted from the druids. Romanus wore the tonsure attributed to Peter: a ring of hair round a shaved centre, symbolizing Christ's crown of thorns. Aidan is said to have given Utta a phial of oil to pour on the waves when a storm rose. There must have been troubled waters of another kind.

Easter was particularly significant for Eanfled. She was born on the Easter Day when her father was saved from assassination. It was also one of the major points of contention between the Celtic and Roman traditions. The contrast at the Northumbrian court was unavoidable. Some years, their Easters fell on different dates, and consequently half their Christian year was out of step. The queen would still be observing

44

Lenten fast while the king was celebrating the Easter feast. Holy Week, Ascension, Pentecost all diverged. Fortunately palaces had several halls, so they could eat separately.

There was still expatriate leadership on both sides: Aidan and the predominantly Irish monks on Lindisfarne, following Columba's tradition, the Italians Romanus and James the Deacon supporting Rome. But a growing number of the players in this drama of the Church were English. Northumbria was the place where soon they would have to decide which model they wanted for their Anglo-Saxon Church. But such was the love and respect both sides had for Aidan, that no one raised the question openly while he was alive.

HILD

Hild was cousin to both King Oswy and Queen Eanfled. She had been baptized by Paulinus. At Oswald Bright-Arm's court she fell in love with Celtic Christianity. Aidan was her spiritual adviser.

Hild was deeply influenced by Lindisfarne. Iona and Ireland had daughter houses for nuns. Tata had her abbey in Kent. Across the Channel there were double houses open to both men and women. English girls from noble families were sent there for education and some remained as nuns. But there was no abbey in Northumbria for women.

Hild's sister Hereswith married a brother of King Anna of East Anglia. After his death, she followed a path common to Christian widows and became a nun. In the absence of a suitable East Anglian abbey, Hereswith went to Chelles, a double house near Paris. Hild decided to follow her there and take the veil.

It was not a retreat from the world. A monastic life opened up possibilities of scholarship, teaching, medical work and community politics. A well-connected abbess did not shut herself away from the world. Long hours were gladly spent in communal worship and private prayer, but these women were also consulted by anyone from kings to cowherds. They were the wise women of their people.

Hild had only got as far as East Anglia when a letter arrived for her from Aidan. He had at last realized the need he had overlooked. In Hild's absence, he had given the veil to Heiu, the first English Northumbrian nun. He had installed her as abbess in her own monastery on the cliffs at Hartlepool. He asked Hild to come back and become a nun in her own country. She responded readily.

Soon she was heading a small community of her own, on the banks of the River Wear. It was not a success. She retreated to Hartlepool.

When Heiu went south to found another abbey in Deira, Hild took her place as abbess. In those days, each abbot devised their own Rule. It owed much to the tradition of the mother house and the advice of the abbot's spiritual director. But there was room for personal initiative. Hartlepool had apparently not been well regulated under Heiu. Hild drew up her own Rule, with Aidan's help. There was a bond of affection and respect between Aidan and Hild. He visited her often, both giving and seeking advice.

At Hartlepool, Hild was 'Mother' to a community of men and women. Mixed monasteries in the English kingdoms were always headed by a woman. Hild was operating in an area where Celtic Christianity was now the norm. Diocesan bishops had ceased to be the most important figures in church government. The abbot of a monastery now occupied that position. Some abbots were bishops too. Aidan was both abbot of Lindisfarne and bishop to the Northumbrians. But others, like Columba of Iona, were not. It was not necessary for an abbot to be a priest, and women could not be. Bishops were still needed, to consecrate priests and confirm new Christians, but they were part of the abbey's staff, not necessarily its head. Hild's position as abbess was higher than a bishop's, as long as the values of Celtic Christianity held.

OSWIN AND OSWY

Aidan had a great affection for Oswy's cousin, King Oswin of Deira. Oswin was a popular man, handsome and courteous. He gave Aidan the best horse from his stable, with rich harness, so that the bishop could cross rivers more easily and cover the ground faster as he visited his far-flung flock. Aidan protested he would rather walk. Finally he submitted reluctantly, but the first time he met a beggar, he dismounted and handed over his mount, complete with gilded trappings.

Oswin had just come in from hunting when he heard the news. He was furious. 'Why didn't you tell me you were going to give it away to a beggar? I needn't have given you my best horse.' Aidan reproached him. 'Is a child of God of less value to you than that four-footed animal?' The meal was about to start and the others went to their seats. But Oswin still stood in front of the fire, chewing his lip, his face angry. Then, with a rush of remorse, he unbuckled his sword and knelt at Aidan's feet. 'I'm sorry. I'll never again question what you do with any gift of mine.' Over the meal, the king was merry now, but Aidan's chaplain saw tears on his abbot's face. Discreetly, using the Irish tongue, he asked him why. Aidan replied, 'He's too good and humble a man to last long as king.' He was right.

King Oswy of Bernicia was of a different temper. He could not accept Penda's authority. His warband harried the Mercians, provoking punishment raids. Penda bypassed the Bernician army and reached Bamburgh. His soldiers tore down the nearby cottages and stacked the beams, wattle panels and thatch from the roofs against the fortress walls. Aidan, following Celtic custom, was in solitary Lenten retreat on the little island of Farne two miles off Bamburgh. He saw the smoke rising from the crag and threw his energies into prayer. The wind changed, blowing in from the sea. Flames and smoke rolled down on the besiegers, burning some and panicking the rest into retreat.

Oswy decided he had had enough. First he made a bid to regain Deira. His peace-loving cousin reluctantly led his army out near Catterick, but when he saw the Bernicians coming, he fled. He and a loyal soldier found refuge in the house of an old friend. But the Deiran thane despised his king for cowardice. He betrayed him to Oswy of Bernicia. Both King Oswin of Deira and his companion were executed.

Eleven days later, Aidan died. He was seated outside the church at Bamburgh, in the shelter of its wall. He had refused the pleas of his monks to let them carry him back to Lindisfarne. It might have been coincidence that he died there, below King Oswy's Bernician fortress. Some said the fever was caused by a broken heart. But he may have engaged in the Celtic practice of fasting outside the gates of a wrongdoer, to compel Oswy to admit his guilt.

At Queen Eanfled's insistence, King Oswy founded a monastery at Gilling, where her kinsman had been executed. Here prayers were offered for the dead king's soul and Oswy's.

Aidan had been loved and respected from Iona to Canterbury. The example of Northumbria, of East Anglia, of Wessex, showed that the two traditions of Celtic and Roman Christianity could co-exist. Their theology was the same. Arguments about their different practices were largely carried out by Celts and Italians over the heads of the Anglo-Saxons. But before Aidan died, the tide had begun to turn with the arrival on Lindisfarne of a teenage boy, Wilfrid.

5

Wilfrid, Cuthbert and the Synod of Whitby

WILFRID'S BOYHOOD

In the year Lindisfarne was founded, two Northumbrian boys were born who symbolize the difference between Roman and Celtic Christianity. Their difference of lifestyle and underlying values went much deeper than the date for Easter or the monks' tonsure.

Wilfrid was the son of a nobleman, a handsome, intelligent lad. He attracted deep affection and devotion from some, implacable hostility from others. He waited on his father's visitors, from noble to slave, and won their good reports. But he was ill-treated by his stepmother.

At 14, he left home and set out for court, splendidly equipped. It was not to King Oswy that Wilfrid presented himself, but Queen Eanfled, asking her help in entering a religious life. In 648, the only option available in Northumbria was a Celtic abbey. One of Oswy's personal bodyguard, Cudda, had suffered paralysis and decided to end his days as a monk on Lindisfarne. Young Wilfrid agreed to accompany him as his personal attendant.

The abbey was physically a poor place, wattle and clay huts around a church with a leaking roof. Its treasures were books, the cattle whose skins provided vellum for new ones, the furnishings of its church and the quality of worship and living of its monks. Celtic worship could be accompanied by beautifully worked vestments, brilliant lamps, illuminated Gospels, but outside the church, life was frugal. Wilfrid drew admiration from both seniors and contemporaries for the diligence with which he carried out his duties to Cudda. He devoted the rest of his time to religious studies. He stayed there four years, but he did not seek the monk's tonsure.

LYON AND ROME

Aidan was succeeded by another Irishman, of a very different temperament. Princess Fina, of the royal house of Ulster, had borne Oswy a son out of wedlock. Her brother Finan came as the second abbot of Lindisfarne and bishop to the Northumbrians. He was a hot-tempered man, sure of his own opinions. In 633, the southern Irish kingdoms had voted to conform to Roman practices. The north of Ireland, together with Columba's Scottish and Pictish churches, held to what they believed to be the ancient, true tradition. A southern Irishman came to Lindisfarne and hotly disputed the matter with Finan. The English must have listened to this controversy with some bewilderment. The choice for them had been between Anglo-Saxon heathenism and Christianity. Now they were being required to take sides over two different expressions of Christianity.

Wilfrid heard this controversy. His reading in Lindisfarne's library fired him with the desire to see Rome for himself. Cudda released him and Queen Eanfled equipped him for the journey to Kent. Her nephew Eorconbert was now king there. Eorconbert was a zealous Christian. He ordered all the remaining idols in Kent to be destroyed and laid down penalties for anyone who broke the fast of Lent. He welcomed Wilfrid but made the 19-year-old wait for a suitable escort. Wilfrid spent a year in Canterbury, studying in the abbey library and observing a monkish discipline.

In 653, another Northumbrian arrived. Biscop Baducing was one of Oswy's bodyguard. The king offered him the customary grant of land at 25, to enable him to marry. Biscop refused. He too wanted to travel to Rome, hungry to learn. Wilfrid was a cheerful, sociable lad; Biscop intelligent, but austere. Even as a boy, he is said to have behaved like an old man. Eorconbert judged him capable of looking after Wilfrid and sent the two on their way with money and recommendations.

They came to the city of Lyon in Gaul, ruled by Count Dalfinus and his brother, Archbishop Annemund. Wilfrid was overwhelmed by its magnificence. Though Annemund lived simply, using his palace as a monastery, worship at Lyon centred on the dazzling church of St Just, with gilded ceiling, coloured marble and stained-glass windows. On feast days, there were magnificent ecclesiastical processions through the streets. It was a surreal contrast to the barefoot walk across wet sands to Lindisfarne and the church Finan had rebuilt with oak planks.

Annemund and Dalfinus took him to their hearts. Annemund wanted to adopt him as his heir, Dalfinus offered him the hand of his daughter and a portion of his territory to govern. Biscop insisted they press on to Rome. They parted. It was a year before Wilfrid followed, promising to return to Lyon.

In the monastery of St Andrew's on the Caelian Hill in Rome, starting point for Augustine's mission, Wilfrid knelt at the altar, where splendid volumes of the four Gospels were displayed. He found a teacher. Archdeacon Boniface had the private ear of the pope. As well as learning the Gospels by heart, Wilfrid was inducted into the grounds for Rome's disagreement with the Celtic churches and emerged passionate in his loyalty to the see of St Peter. The pope Eugenius granted Wilfrid an audience and gave him gifts of holy relics to take back to Britain.

Returning to Lyon, Wilfrid was welcomed enthusiastically by Annemund. Here, safe from the Celtic taint of Lindisfarne, he became a monk and received the Roman tonsure.

His three years' stay ended dramatically. The local bishops attracted the enmity of the queen-regent Baldhild, an English slave who had married a Frankish king and ended her life as an abbess. Annemund was arrested and sentenced to death. Wilfrid declared his intention of following him to martyrdom. He too stripped for execution. The astonished judges inquired who this fair-haired foreigner was. Hearing he was English, they told him this quarrel was nothing to do with him and sent him home.

CUTHBERT

If Wilfrid was attracted to the centre, Cuthbert felt the lure of the fringe. His parents were not noble, though they kept servants and horses. Cuthbert was a high-spirited lad, whose energy left him standing on the field looking for a playmate when all the other children had retired exhausted. Like the other boys, he used to stand on his head, his tunic falling to reveal his bare bottom. He reportedly sobered up when an infant reproached him for behaviour inappropriate in a future bishop. At eight, he was sent to a foster-mother, Kenswith. She was a devout woman and it was a loving relationship. Cuthbert continued to visit her through his adult life.

He grew tall and strong, doing military service and learning to live on meagre rations. His foster-mother's teaching and his own natural courage came into play when he witnessed a drama on the River Wear. Monks from a community on the south shore were gathering timber upstream. They lashed them into rafts and were poling them downriver when a gale sprang up. Rescue boats put out from the monastery but were beaten back. The monks were swept out to sea, until they looked no bigger than five birds. On the north bank, a crowd jeered at them. Cuthbert strode in among them and asked why they were not praying for the men's safety. The Northumbrians complained that these Christians were upsetting society. No one knew what to believe any more. Cuthbert flung himself on his knees and began to pray. The wind dropped and the rafts came safe to harbour. A change came over the hostile crowd. Witnesses remembered afterwards the shame they felt in the face of Cuthbert's courage and compassion.

Cuthbert was 17 when he was up on the hills one night, working as a shepherd. He saw a vision of angels carrying a brilliant soul up a ladder to heaven. Next morning, the news of Aidan's death confirmed his vocation to become a monk. He handed the sheep back to their owners and set out on horseback, with a spear and a single servant. He made for Melrose, a daughter monastery of Lindisfarne. Its abbot, Eata, was one of the first 12 English students in Aidan's school. At the gate, Cuthbert was greeted by the prior, Boisil. They formed a lifelong friendship, as teacher and pupil.

Cuthbert became known for his energy and hardihood. He undertook strenuous missionary journeys into remote hill country. He made contact with villagers so violent and uncivilized that others were afraid to approach them. He was away for a week, a fortnight, even a month, travelling on horseback or on foot. He exercised a stern discipline of fasting and vigils, and drank no alcohol, but he was sensible enough not to tax his body beyond the point where his physical stamina would be weakened.

He was travelling with a boy as companion when they found themselves without food and out of sight of habitation. They watched an eagle drop a fish by a stream. 'Run and get it,' urged Cuthbert. The boy returned proudly with his find, to be reproached by Cuthbert. 'Doesn't the servant who provided it for us deserve a share? Go back and give her half.'

THE MISSION TO MIDDLE ENGLAND

South of Bernicia lay Deira. If King Oswy hoped the murder of his cousin would bring him rule over it, he was disappointed. Penda placed Oswald Bright-Arm's son, now grown to manhood, as client-king. On the other side of the Humber lay heathen Mercia and the sub-kingdom of the Middle Angles. Penda sought to bind Oswy's loyalty by taking his young son by Eanfled as hostage, and arranging marriages between his own children and the children of Oswy's first marriage.

Whole kingdoms were changed by Christian princesses. Alchfled, daughter of Oswy and a British princess, knew her duty. She was to marry Penda's son Peada, sub-king of the Middle Angles. Alchfled raised the stakes usually demanded by such brides. She would not marry Peada unless he became a Christian. Her prospective father-in-law's hostility to Christianity must have mellowed with age. He is said to have despised insincerity more. His son agreed to undergo instruction on Lindisfarne. The holy island worked its miracle. When Peada had completed the course, he declared he would have embraced Christianity, even if it had not won him Alchfled. He was baptized by Finan in the River Tyne, near Newcastle, with his companions and household.

Riding south, the couple brought four priests from Lindisfarne. Diuma was Irish. The other three were English: including Cedd, another of Aidan's first 12 students. That early school was bearing fruit. The Middle Angles responded to their Christian message.

CEDD AND THE EAST SAXONS

But Cedd did not stay long in the midlands. The East Saxons had been staunchly heathen for 40 years, since Mellitus's expulsion. Now King Sigbert of Essex became friendly with Oswy of Northumbria. When Sigbert visited Bamburgh, Oswy persuaded him of the folly of worshipping idols carved from wood. Sigbert accepted Christianity and was baptized in the Tyne. He asked for a missionary for the East Saxons. Oswy recalled Cedd from Middle England and despatched him to Essex with another priest.

They founded two monasteries and a school, transforming untutored heathen East Saxons into monks. The church at Bradwell-on-Sea may date from Cedd's time. It was built in the Kentish style, of stone salvaged from Roman ruins. Cedd returned to Northumbria to report progress and was consecrated bishop to the East Saxons.

Sigbert of Essex suffered a similar fate to his namesake, the king of East Anglia, who had refused to arm himself with more than his staff. Cedd warned the East Saxon king to avoid the house of an excommunicated kinsman. Sigbert ignored the prohibition. The nobleman and his brother assassinated him. The excuse the guilty pair offered was that Sigbert was too ready to forgive anyone who asked him and too lenient to his enemies. The spirituality of the Sermon on the Mount overturned the heroic values of Anglo-Saxon heathenism. More often, though, Christian kings were as violent as their forebears. The God of Old Testament battles was more understandable to them than the Servant Christ.

Cedd often returned to Northumbria. His brother Caelin was chaplain to Oswald Bright-Arm's son, King Oethelwald of Deira. Oethelwald offered Cedd land for an abbey. Lastingham was in the hills, but within reach of York. The king wanted

Cedd to visit the court and advise him, and would himself pray at the abbey and be buried there. The Anglo-Celtic Church favoured wild settings, for solitary communion with God. But these abbots were not isolated from the world and were prepared to upbraid kings whom they believed to be transgressing God's law.

Cedd determined to consecrate the land before building. He began a Lenten fast, eating nothing until evening, and then only milk, bread and a hen's egg, except on Sundays. Before the end of Lent, Oethelwald sent for him. Cedd's duty was to act as the king's soul-friend, but this vigil was also important. He asked a third brother, Cynibil, to complete the fast in his place. The fourth, Chad, was away studying in Ireland.

THE CONVERSION OF MERCIA

Oswy chafed at his subjection to Mercia. He made a vow. If he defeated Penda, he would give the Church 12 estates for monasteries, and his baby daughter. In 654, at a battlefield near Leeds, the River Winwaed surged down in flood. More of Penda's troops were drowned than killed by weapons. The almost 80-year-old heathen king, who had subjugated so much of Britain, lay dead.

Oswy and his Christian son-in-law Peada now ruled the midlands. The Irishman Diuma, who had accompanied Alchfled on her marriage, was consecrated bishop to the peoples of Mercia, Middle England and Lindsey. Diuma founded a double monastery at Repton. Oswy and Peada granted land for the building of a great abbey at Peterborough. Northumbrian influence, and the Anglo-Celtic Church, extended as far south as the Thames.

Within months, Peada was murdered. After two years of uncertainty, three noblemen produced another of Penda's sons out of hiding. They led a successful rebellion against Northumbrian rule and placed Wulfhere on the throne. Wulfhere was a Christian and independent Mercia proved every bit as much committed to the Church's cause. Wulfhere, his brother and two sisters added their signatures to Oswy's when Peterborough's abbey was dedicated.

In Northumbria, Oswy fulfilled his vow. He gave the Church 12 estates, six in Bernicia and six in Deira, both provinces of a reunited kingdom. Each grant comprised ten hides. A hide was a measure of land sufficient to support a family. Individually, the grants were modest. But revenue equivalent to 120 family holdings was shifted from the royal treasury to the Church.

Hild received one estate, known now by its viking name as Whitby. Like Hartlepool, it was the cliff site of a Roman signal station. She moved into her new double abbey in 657. Hild was a notable teacher and preacher; Whitby became famous for its educational ministry. She educated five future bishops, at a time when they were thin on the ground. Some monasteries kept secular dress and preserved social distinctions. At Whitby, there was no personal property. Everyone was expected to study the scriptures and serve others.

Hild was also entrusted with Oswy's and Eanfled's infant daughter, Aelffled, in fulfilment of his vow. Idealistic young adults were choosing the celibate life of the monastery. Others made their way there as a second career, relinquishing their position as household manager or warrior because of widowhood or infirmity. There were also oblates, offered by their parents in childhood, often in response to answered prayer. Whitby was an all-age community of both sexes.

Oswy made his son Alchfrith sub-king of Deira. Alchfrith gave land at Ripon for a new abbey and invited Eata of Melrose south as abbot. Eata brought Cuthbert to be guest-master. Cuthbert washed the feet of travellers, warmed them at his breast on freezing days and fetched the guests food from the kitchen.

The English Advance

Birinus, Wessex's first bishop, died around 650. King Cenwalh received a visit from a Frankish cleric, Agilbert, who had been studying in the monastic schools of Ireland. The king offered him the vacant see of Dorchester-on-Thames. It was not a happy relationship. Agilbert proved unable, or unwilling, to master the English language.

Elsewhere, the English were advancing, not only territorially but in the leadership of the Church. In 644, Honorius of Canterbury consecrated the first English bishop, Ithamar, for the see of Rochester. In East Anglia, the Burgundian Felix was succeeded by Thomas, a fenland Englishman. And in 655, following Honorius's death, the West Saxon Fithlocan became the first English archbishop of Canterbury. The English bishop, Ithamar, consecrated him and he took the religious name Deusdedit. In the north, similar authority was held by abbots and abbesses, like the English Eata and Cedd, Heiu and Hild.

Cenwalh of Wessex drove the Britons beyond the River Parrett in Somerset. The West Saxons gained the holy island of Glastonbury, rising from the meres of the Somerset Levels. There were British monks there. The West Saxons seem to have remained on better terms with the British than was often the case on the frontiers of invasion.

Cenwalh's advance also won the great Selwood Forest. In these tangled woods, an Irish hermit had made his cell. Maildubh attracted many of the English, by his extreme example of a lifestyle devoted to God. Local people went in awe of the evident holiness of hermits. In forests and fens, caves and cliffs, these spiritual athletes survived triumphant over evil spirits, which both heathens and Christians were sure haunted such wildernesses. The hermits were on the side of the people, asking nothing for themselves, giving help and teaching. Their solitude was often lost as a new community formed around them.

Maildubh gathered a school at Malmesbury. Irish scholars came to teach there. To this forest community, a young Englishman, Aldhelm, arrived to study and became one of the most influential writers of the age. Other Irish hermits were worshipping and witnessing elsewhere, certainly in Sussex and East Anglia.

WILFRID'S RETURN

Wilfrid returned in 660 from his long stay in Rome and Lyon, convinced of Rome's authority and dazzled by the magnificence of continental episcopacy. He found a greatly changed Britain.

From being a lone beacon in Northumbria, Celtic Christianity was now a major influence in English lands, from the Scottish borders to the English Channel. It had taken root in Essex. In East Anglia and Wessex, English kings were supporting both continental Catholic bishops and Irish hermit-evangelists. Only Kent was solidly loyal to Augustine's ways. Augustine's mission is often credited with evangelizing England, or even Britain. The reality is that most lasting conversions came from elsewhere. Significantly, early English handwriting was based not on the Italian but the Irish style.

Wilfrid landed in Wessex. King Cenwalh recommended this remarkable young man to his friend Alchfrith of Deira. Alchfrith was enchanted by Wilfrid's tales and impressed by his arguments for the supremacy of Rome. He wanted his new friend at court, asking him endless questions. But Wilfrid, who was not yet a priest, needed a base from which to exercise authority. Alchfrith gave him land for a monastery at Stanford. Then his eye fell on Ripon, daughter house of Melrose. Alchfrith ordered Eata and his monks to change to the Roman monastic tonsure and date of Easter. It was a challenge to the authority of Columba and his churches. Eata refused to change. Alchfrith threw the Anglo-Celtic monks out and gave their abbey to Wilfrid.

CUTHBERT AT MELROSE

Back at Melrose, Cuthbert was reunited with his friend and teacher, the prior Boisil. Illness struck. As Cuthbert lay gravely ill, the brothers kept a night vigil of prayer. When Cuthbert heard about it next morning, he leapt out of bed saying, 'God can't possibly fail to heed the prayers of so many good men.' There is a refreshing honesty about the account. Cuthbert evidently overestimated the speed of his healing; his health was never as robust afterwards.

It was Boisil's turn to succumb. Feeling death approaching, he urged Cuthbert to be quick if he wanted any further teaching from him. They had, at most, a week. 'What can we cover in so short a time?' asked Cuthbert. Boisil had a commentary on St John's Gospel, bound in seven sections. The

Celtic Church honoured the Gospel of John above all others. The friends completed a section a day, leaving aside weighty theology and concentrating on the essence, Christ's message of love. Soon afterwards, Boisil died.

Cuthbert continued to travel the hill country and even voyaged north to the Picts. He visited the clifftop abbey of Coldingham, where Oswy's sister Aebbe had founded a monastery on St Abb's Head. One of the monks discovered that Cuthbert left his bed at night, appearing again in chapel for the dawn service. He trailed Cuthbert to the seashore. Following the practice of Celtic ascetics, Cuthbert walked out into the dark North Sea and stood for hours praying. When he waded back to the beach, two sea-otters came gambolling up. They dried his skin with their fur and rolled themselves around to warm him.

Coldingham was not as well regulated as Whitby. One of Aebbe's monks reported that the others were idling away in gossip the time they should be spending on prayer. The nuns were more interested in making themselves fine dresses than studying scripture. Aebbe tightened the discipline.

AGILBERT

At Ripon, Wilfrid instituted the changes Eata had refused. Ripon was a rich abbey, of 30 hides. Wilfrid's biographer says he was now wealthy enough to give alms to the poor and the sick.

His abbeys were in competition with Anglo-Celtic founda-tions, like Hild's. The old dispute between Italian and Irish missions was becoming an issue for the English Church.

Into this situation came two more foreigners. Finan died in 661. The new abbot of Lindisfarne was Colman, another Irishman, trained on Iona. In Wessex, King Cenwalh lost patience with the Frankish bishop Agilbert's mutilations of the English language. He appealed to Canterbury. They sent an Englishman, Wini, priested in Gaul. Cenwalh divided Wessex into two dioceses and installed the newcomer at Winchester. Agilbert was so insulted at losing half his see that he packed his bags and left.

Agilbert came to Deira, and found its sub-king sympathetic. Alchfrith introduced him to his protégé Wilfrid and asked Agilbert to ordain him priest. Wilfrid would never have sought ordination from a Celtic bishop. He accepted priesthood from the Catholic Agilbert.

THE SYNOD OF WHITBY

It was Wilfrid's single-mindedness which ended co-existence. In 664, one of those years when Celtic and Roman Easters differed, Alchfrith called a synod of the Deiran Church, to decide whether Roman or Celtic usage should prevail. Then Oswy stepped in, as king of all Northumbria. He distrusted his son's loyalty. He was not going to see Alchfrith split the country over this issue. This synod would be for Bernicia as well as Deira. It was to be held at Hild's abbey of Whitby and Oswy would chair it.

On the Celtic side were the king, raised on Iona, Colman, abbot-bishop of Lindisfarne, Hild, abbess of Whitby and Cedd, abbot of Lastingham and bishop to the East Saxons, with their supporters.

The Romans counted the Italian chaplain Romanus, representing Queen Eanfled, the visiting Frankish bishop Agilbert with his chaplain, Abbot Wilfrid, and James the Deacon, the surviving link with Paulinus's mission. The Roman Church had been less successful here in supplying English leaders. Still, the Irish and Frankish bishops would be pitted against each other as chief spokesmen. The Anglo-Celtic side must have relished the prospect of Agilbert's problems with the English language. Cedd would act as interpreter.

Oswy invited Colman to make his opening speech. He pleaded ancient tradition, the authority of St John, confirmed by Columba. The king turned to the Roman side. Agilbert overturned all expectations. He asked for permission to hand over Rome's case to Wilfrid, who could address them in English.

The change was devastating. Wilfrid had a quick mind and a fluent tongue. He had studied these matters in Rome. The calculation of the date of Easter was immensely complicated. Tables had been drawn up and revised over the centuries. It hardly mattered that both sides misunderstood the arithmetic. What was really at issue was the basis of authority.

Wilfrid pointed out that St John had celebrated Easter on a weekday. Having demolished one beloved authority, he went on to dismiss Columba as an ignorant monk at the remotest edge of the world. If Iona's founder had known what was accepted in Rome, Jerusalem, Antioch, Alexandria, and not conformed, he would be unworthy to be counted a Christian.

Colman was appalled. To the monks of Lindisfarne, Columba was next to Christ. He could find no answer to what was, for him, near blasphemy. Others must have spoken, but their speeches are not recorded. Wilfrid cited St Peter, who held the keys of heaven, implying that any bishop of Rome inherited complete authority. Oswy asked the assembly if the quotation was true. They answered unanimously, yes. In that case, Oswy declared, he dared not decide against Rome, lest at his death St Peter should refuse to open the gate of heaven for him.

Northumbria remained united. The price was that Lindisfarne, and its daughter churches, must renounce Celtic traditions. The reality was that the Celtic spirit persisted within the English churches long after Whitby.

6

Towards a National Church

CHANGE AT LINDISFARNE

Heartbroken, Colman left Lindisfarne and returned to Iona. Many monks went with him, including 30 Englishmen. They moved on to Ireland and set up a new community on Inishboffin, off the west coast. But the ethnic groups fell out. The Irish monks took off for the hills in the summer, leaving the English to work the island fields. Colman settled the matter by founding a new community for them on the mainland. Eventually, it conformed to Roman practice. It received a succession of English bishops in the eighth century and was represented at English synods. For centuries it remained 'Mayo of the Saxons'.

The roles of abbot of Lindisfarne and bishop to the Northumbrians were separated. Power would shift to bishops. If Wilfrid had hoped for the new bishopric, he was disappointed. It went to another Englishman, trained in Ireland. At Colman's request, Oswy gave the abbacy to Eata of Melrose, the man Wilfrid had ousted from Ripon. It must have been an emotive moment to cross the sands as the first English abbot of Lindisfarne, where he had come as a boy to Aidan's new school.

He brought Cuthbert with him as prior, responsible for community discipline. Eata and Cuthbert accepted the verdict of the synod and implemented the Roman practices they had once refused. It was not easy. Many monks who stayed resented the changes. There were heated chapter meetings. Cuthbert was not a man for violent argument. When his patience gave out, he got up and left. He walked the island, clearing his head with the sea breeze and chatting with workers in the fields, singing psalms as he shared their labour. Next day, he repeated the requirements. He drew up a written Rule for Lindisfarne, replacing Aidan's informal tradition. He remained outwardly cheerful, except when he celebrated mass, when the immensity of Christ's sacrifice reduced him to tears.

PLAGUE

The year of the Synod of Whitby, plague swept the country. Cedd died at Lastingham. When his community in Essex heard, they came north in a body, determined to follow their beloved abbot. Most died. Cedd's place at Lastingham was filled by his brother Chad, another of those original 12 students.

In Essex, without leadership Christianity faltered. Overwhelmed with deaths from plague, one ruler reverted to heathenism, along with many of his people. The other held firm to his faith. Wulfhere of Mercia saved the day. He sent Bishop Jaruman, whose diligent travels persuaded the apostates to abandon or destroy their temples and reopen the churches.

Egbert was one who left Northumbria in protest after the Synod of Whitby. He joined the host of English students seeking learning in Ireland, where monasteries gave free board and lodging and the loan of books. Egbert watched his companions dying of plague around him, even his cell-mate. He vowed that, if he was spared, he would devote his life to God in exile. When he alone survived, he became an indefatigable campaigner for the Roman changes. It was he who finally persuaded Iona to conform.

Archbishop Deusdedit of Canterbury died in the plague. So did the newly appointed bishop to the Northumbrians. Wilfrid now got his chance. King Oswy offered him the bishopric.

This presented Wilfrid with a difficulty. It was going to be hard to find three bishops, untainted by Celtic irregularity, to perform his consecration. He went to Gaul, where Agilbert was now bishop of Paris. The ceremony was all that Wilfrid would have wished. Twelve bishops carried him through the cathedral in a golden chair.

But Wilfrid stayed too long. After two years, Oswy lost patience and appointed Chad bishop, with his see at York.

Chad went to Canterbury for consecration, but found it still lacking an archbishop. He travelled on to Wessex, where Wini of Winchester consecrated him. Wini was assisted by two British bishops, probably from the south-west kingdom of Dumnonia. Neither Chad nor Wini questioned the validity of Celtic episcopacy.

Wilfrid, returning from his glorious consecration, was furious. He questioned everything about Chad's appointment: the king's high-handed change of mind, the fact that two of the bishops involved were, in Wilfrid's opinion, not properly consecrated themselves, and the authority of the king to act in the Church's affairs. He appealed to Canterbury.

THEODORE

After Deusdedit, another Englishman, Wighard, was chosen for archbishop by all the English churches, King Oswy of Northumbria and King Egbert of Kent. They wanted an archbishop who spoke the language of the people. Wighard was sent for consecration to the pope himself, evidence of the shortage of acceptable English bishops. He presented his credentials in Rome, but died of plague before the ceremony could be performed. Pope Vitalian felt responsible for providing a successor. He did not consult the English Church.

He chose Hadrian, a North African abbot. Hadrian protested he was unworthy, but recommended his friend Theodore, a refugee from Arab-occupied Tarsus. Theodore was already 66, but a remarkably able man. He had been tonsured in the Greek style, not the Roman. Pope Vitalian insisted he wait until it grew out and could be recut. Tonsures symbolized deeper differences. There was controversy between eastern and western Churches, on theology as well as practice. Theodore was warned not to introduce dubious Greek customs into the English Church.

Hadrian did not escape. Vitalian sent him to act as Theodore's minder and ensure sound Catholic doctrine. Both were outstanding scholars.

They took as guide and interpreter Wilfrid's old travelling companion. Biscop Baducing had returned to study in Rome and was tonsured at the teaching abbey of Lérins, off the south coast of France. He took the religious name of Benedict and was known as Benedict Biscop.

In Paris, Hadrian was arrested on suspicion of spying. When he eventually reached Kent, Theodore made him abbot of the monastery of Peter and Paul. These foreign scholars transformed the teaching ministry of Canterbury. The Romans had lost the knowledge of Greek and the wisdom of the eastern schools. This lack was now brilliantly supplied by these two men.

ARCHBISHOP OF THE ENGLISH

Like Gregory, Theodore saw Britain as a single country, over which the archbishop of Canterbury would have ecclesiastical authority. The reality was a patchwork of separate kingdoms, each with its own Church, dependent on the patronage of its king. Though Canterbury appeared to succeed at the Synod of Whitby, Theodore found in 668 only one bishop left south of the Humber. That was Wini, formerly of Winchester. He too had fallen out of favour with King Cenwalh and lost his post. He moved to Mercia and, with King Wulfhere's help, purchased the see of London. This sin of simony was made tempting by the Church's increasing revenue from substantial gifts.

Theodore asserted the right of ecclesiastical over secular power by intervening in the Northumbrian dispute. Chad humbly admitted that he had never thought himself worthy to be a bishop. Theodore upheld Wilfrid's complaints, but rectified the matter of Chad's consecration by laying his own hands on him. A diplomatic solution was found. A new bishop was needed for the midlands. Chad was sent to Lichfield. He set up a hermitage beside a pool. Chad's heart was still with Celtic Christianity. His brother Cedd had ridden on horseback. Chad toured his diocese on foot. When Theodore presented him with a horse, Chad protested. The archbishop bodily hoisted him into the saddle.

In 672, Theodore summoned representatives of the English churches to meet him at a synod in Hertford. He, not the host king, took the chair. It made visible a unity which transcended political barriers, paving the way for England to become one country. British kingdoms were not represented.

A raft of decisions was made. A bishop might not interfere in another diocese. Priests might not leave their parishes without their bishop's consent, nor operate in another diocese without the leave of that bishop. More bishops would be needed. Bishops were forbidden to interfere with abbeys, but the course was set away from monasteries towards diocesan government.

CHURCH BUILDING

Theodore believed a huge diocese like Wilfrid's Northumbria needed to be divided to ensure good pastoral care. Wilfrid was amassing great wealth from gifts of estates. Young nobles came to his household to receive military training. He rode with an armed escort rivalling the king's. We see a new model emerging: the prince-bishop. In Rochester, the new bishop resigned the see because of its poverty.

Oswy was succeeded by his son Ecgfrith, who had been Penda's hostage as a boy. His first queen was Aethelthryth, daughter of the devout King Anna of East Anglia. She was 12 years older, strong-minded in the Anglo-Saxon tradition. She had refused to consummate her brief first marriage and adopted the same policy with Ecgfrith. Wilfrid, her spiritual director, supported her. Ecgfrith promised Wilfrid wealth if he could persuade her to give in. Aethelthryth responded by giving Wilfrid a great estate at Hexham. The royal marriage was dissolved. Wilfrid gave Aethelthryth the veil and she began her new career as a nun at Coldingham, under Ecgfrith's aunt Aebbe.

Two years later, she returned to East Anglia and founded the great double abbey at Ely. She bathed in warm water only before festivals and was always the last of her community to use the bathwater. She died of a neck tumour, which she accepted as an expurgation of the vanity of her youth, when she had worn necklaces of gold and pearls.

Wilfrid threw himself into a major programme of church

building. At York, the stone church Paulinus had begun was a sorry mess. Water streamed through the dilapidated roof. Mould and bird droppings stained everything. Wilfrid used his new wealth to restore it. A more splendid stone church rose at Ripon, Italian building techniques replacing English timbered halls. He beautified it with gold, silver and purple, and had an illuminated Gospel book made, with letters of gold on purple vellum. He dedicated this new church in a magnificent ceremony in the presence of kings, nobility and church dignitaries. From the chancel steps he read out the list of British church lands confiscated by the English, which the king had handed over to him. Then he entertained his guests to a three-day feast.

In 672 he began building at Hexham. He used stone from the Roman ruins of Corbridge for its massive walls, columns, spiral stairs and crypt.

For his part, Benedict Biscop made another journey to Rome and returned laden with precious books. Benedict's enthusiasm convinced Ecgfrith to give him land at Wearmouth for the monastery of St Peter. Benedict crossed the sea again in search of stonemasons. He fetched glaziers from France and set them teaching their craft to the English.

WILFRID IN EXILE

Ecgfrith's second queen was as antagonistic to Wilfrid as Aethelthryth had been favourable. Iurminburg impressed upon the king the challenge posed by the bishop's vast landholding, extensive buildings, and the large armed retinue which attended him in livery which would not disgrace a king. Theodore wanted to divide the Northumbrian diocese. Wilfrid would not hear of sharing power. King Ecgfrith seized the opportunity, stripped Wilfrid of his bishopric and estates and expelled him, with Theodore's concurrence. Wilfrid claimed furiously that he was defrauded of his wealth. He took his grievance over the heads of king and archbishop, to Rome.

In Rome, the defence was representing Theodore and Hild, who was still a respected authority in Northumbria. But Wilfrid's charismatic presence convinced the council. He was to be restored to his see, and the monasteries of Ripon and Hexham returned to him. His diocese would still be divided, but he could choose his suffragans.

Time and again throughout his life, Wilfrid appealed to central authority, achieved a favourable verdict, and returned to antagonize a succession of kings and queens, churchmen and churchwomen. He lost office and estates again, spent months in a windowless dungeon, years in exile. He returned to house arrest. At one time, only Sussex, the last heathen English kingdom, would have him.

But Wilfrid was man of dynamic courage and zeal. Driven ashore on the Sussex coast, he battled with violent looters, while a heathen priest chanted spells of binding. When he was blown on to the Frisian coast and found himself again among heathens, he stayed for while evangelizing them. As an exile in Sussex, he set about converting them too. His credibility was enhanced when he relieved a famine by teaching them to fish with nets. When their Christian king gave him an estate at Selsey, Wilfrid baptized 250 slaves and freed them.

Wilfrid attracted huge loyalty as well as enmity. He amassed gifts. Abbots put their monasteries under his protection and made him their heir. But he was his own worst enemy. A less contentious diocesan might have achieved Gregory's vision of an archbishopric for York by now.

CAEDMON

Theodore and Benedict Biscop both enthusiastically promoted liturgical singing. They introduced music teachers. Arch-cantor John came from Rome to teach the detailed celebration of festivals through the church year, but also to check on Theodore's orthodoxy.

In 680, a new talent was revealed at Whitby. When the lute passed round the hall, Caedmon always got up and left before it was his turn to give the company a song. He may have lacked musical talent or been shocked by the heathen and lewd nature of much Anglo-Saxon song. All religious poetry was in Latin, which, like most Anglo-Saxon laymen, Caedmon did not know.

On one such evening, he slipped away early to the cow-shed. While he slept, he heard a man commanding him to sing. 'I can't,' he protested. 'That's why I'm out here.' The man persisted. 'But what am I supposed to sing about?' 'Sing of the making of the universe,' was the startling reply. Caedmon found a great song of creation swelling through his dreams, not in Latin, but in Anglo-Saxon. Next morning, he told his foreman. The man took him straight to the monastery and he sang it to the chapter. They saw at once the potential for communicating Christianity to a lay audience. Another passage of scripture was produced, and translated for him. Caedmon returned with another English poem of praise. He became a monk. Before long, he had composed a repertoire of Anglo-Saxon song, telling the whole story of salvation.

From Hermit to Bishop

Cuthbert retired from Lindisfarne to live the life of a hermit on Inner Farne. He insisted this was not a higher calling. It was harder to live in community.

He hollowed a little house out of the rock, dragging huge boulders for walls. It had one side window, through which he blessed pilgrims and received necessities. As time went on he shuttered that and saw only the sky. He grew a little barley. Monks sailed the nine miles from Lindisfarne to augment his supplies, staying at a guesthouse by the landing place. When he scolded two crows for stealing the thatch, they returned carrying pig lard. Cuthbert recommended visitors to grease their boots with it. His own boots were only removed on Maundy Thursday, revealing the calluses on his shins from countless genuflections.

Theodore had divided Wilfrid's diocese into two. In 684, he decided Bernicia needed another bishop. Cuthbert, beloved by all, was judged the right man. Messengers were sent to Farne, but Cuthbert repeatedly refused, begging to be left solitary. At last King Ecgfrith and the bishop of Abercorn were rowed out to plead with him. Cuthbert came in tears. The intention was to create him bishop of Hexham, but Eata took the compassionate decision to change places, so that Cuthbert could at least remain on Lindisfarne.

Cuthbert took his responsibilities seriously. It was a bishop's duty to tour his diocese annually. Cuthbert's visits took him to the Roman city of Carlisle, the hill country, where he and his retinue slept in tents, to monks and nuns and the estates of nobles. He entered a village devastated by plague and kissed a diseased infant in its frantic mother's arms.

ALDFRITH THE WISE

Oswy's daughter Aelffled was now abbess of Whitby, where Hild had brought her as an infant. In 684, she summoned Cuthbert to meet her on Coquet Island. She was concerned about who would rule Northumbria when her childless brother Ecgfrith died. Cuthbert told her the new king would also be a brother. Look at these islands. Could God not summon a king from such an isle? Aelffled realized he meant her illegitimate half-brother Aldfrith, then on Iona.

Next year, Ecgfrith attacked the Picts, ignoring Cuthbert's warning. He was killed, with great losses among his warhost. The size and power of Northumbria was severely reduced. It lost the monastery and bishopric of Abercorn.

But it gained a king like no other of his time. Aldfrith was Oswy's son by the Irish princess Fina. To the Irish he was Flann Fina, 'Blood of the Wine'. He had never expected to be king and his education suggests a vocation to the priesthood. As a young man, he was a fellow student of the monk Aldhelm, at Malmesbury or Canterbury. Aldhelm became his godfather and the two enjoyed a literary correspondence. Aldfrith was heir to Irish enthusiasm for learning and was one of the best-read people in his kingdom. He wrote poetry in Latin, Anglo-Saxon and Irish.

He was on Iona when his brother Ecgfrith's body was brought there to be buried. The Synod of Whitby had not severed the link between Columba's island and Northumbria.

In Aldfrith's reign scholarship flourished. The abbot of Iona gave him a copy of his book on the Holy Places, gleaned from a pilgrim driven ashore in the Hebrides. Aldfrith circulated it around his kingdom. He paid for a rare book he wanted, on cosmography, with a large grant of land to Wearmouth monastery.

Aldfrith found a fellow enthusiast in Benedict Biscop. In 685, Wearmouth's sister abbey of Jarrow was dedicated, a few miles from the original house. The twin monasteries worked as one. Benedict always returned from his frequent trips abroad laden with books, relics and religious pictures. Wearmouth and Jarrow had stone buildings and stained-glass windows, but these were not their greatest glory. Benedict made them into a cultural centre unrivalled outside Rome. As he lay dying, one of his greatest concerns was that his marvellous library should not be split up.

CUTHBERT'S DEATH

In the winter of 686, Cuthbert knew he was dying, probably of tuberculosis. He returned to his beloved hermitage on Farne. The abbot himself attended him but when duty called him back to Lindisfarne, Cuthbert insisted on remaining alone. Bad weather kept the monks away for five days. When they returned, Cuthbert had dragged himself down to the guest-house on his ulcerated foot. He drew back the blanket and showed them five onions he had brought for food. Only one was nibbled. He allowed them to carry him back to his hut, where no one but he had entered for years, and there he died.

Cuthbert wanted to be buried, and rise again, on Farne. He had a sarcophagus and shroud ready. But when the monks on Lindisfarne saw the torch signal telling that his spirit had passed, they brought his body back to the mother abbey and interred him reverently there. A year later, his body was exhumed and transferred to a tomb beside the altar, a recognition of sainthood. He was dressed in splendid priestly vestments of Byzantine silk, with the pectoral cross of gold and garnet he had worn as a bishop. Cuthbert was a deeply humble and spiritual man. Yet he accepted the dignity of ecclesiastical office.

Cuthbert was an Englishman. He died a diocesan bishop, wearing the Roman tonsure. He anathematized on his deathbed schismatics who would break the peace of the Church. Yet he remains an inspirational representative of Anglo-Celtic spirituality, the hermit whose holiness does not allow him to remain in the solitude he seeks with God, but serves the needs of God's people and attracts their love. He showed both strands could be woven into Anglo-Saxon Christianity.

LAWS AND THE CHURCH

Theodore died in 690. He had brought order to the diverse and disunited English churches. His penitentials reflect the violent times and his compassion for those whose lives were torn apart. He deals with the situation when a partner has been carried into captivity with no hope of return. And what if they should come back, against all odds? What if one partner enters a life of religion, is taken into slavery, or deserts their spouse? He is on the side of humanity, rather than the absolute indissolubility of marriage.

A century after Gregory saw those English boys in Rome, all the English kingdoms were led by Christian kings. The Church was acting as a unifying force for the English kingdoms. It was also making an impression on law codes, reinforcing the power of the Church.

King Ine inherited the expanding kingdom of Wessex, with its patchwork of missions and monasteries. Ine summoned the first West Saxon synod, at which he presided. He listened to the advice of both clergy and nobles, and gave his own. Around 694, he drew up a code of law. Children must be baptized within 30 days. There was a tax of 'church scot' to finance the Church's work. Work on Sunday was punished by enslavement. On the other hand, a slave whose owner forced them to labour on Sunday could claim freedom.

Slavery was rooted deep, in ecclesiastical society as well as lay. The manumission, or legal freeing, of slaves was recommended by the Church as beneficial to the soul, but keeping slaves was not a sin. Early in the eighth century, the archbishop of Canterbury writes a touching letter to the bishop of Sherborne. He asks him to renew pressure on the abbot of Glastonbury to release a Kentish girl, sister of the man bearing this letter. The abbot has so far rejected pleas to return this captive to her family. The archbishop offers to pay a high ransom for her.

Ine's queen felt her husband was too wedded to earthly joys. After a particularly riotous country house weekend, she is said to have stopped the royal cavalcade after only a mile. She begged him, with fond endearments, to go back with her. He readily gave in. To his horror, he found the palace fouled with cow dung and filth. She led him to their bed. There lay a sow which had just farrowed. 'Now,' she asked, 'where are the oriental tapestries, the gold dishes, the rare delicacies, of yesterday? Look how our pampered bodies decay.' The king took heed. Ine became a deeply religious man. He restored the abbey at Glastonbury, now refounded with English monks. He built a new church, but preserved the ancient wattle one. Towards the end of his life he and his wife went to Rome. Ine was shaved like a monk and put on a humble habit. They lived their last years in pious retirement.

In 695 King Wihtred of Kent, helped by Aldhelm, abbot of Malmesbury, also drew up a law code giving the Church privileges which rivalled the king's. The Church was to be free from taxation. A later Kentish council freed royal monasteries from the control of the founding family, giving them the right to choose their own abbots, with the bishop's approval.

WEALTH

Wilfrid died in retirement at his monastery of Oundle in 709. In his final tour of his estates and religious foundations, his principal concern was for the disposal of his wealth. He had the treasurer open the diocesan coffers and make four heaps of gold, silver and jewels, personally directing what should be put on each pile. One was to be sent to churches in Rome, another distributed to the poor, a third was for the abbots of Hexham and Ripon, 'to secure the favour of kings and bishops', the fourth went to those who had been loyal to him in exile.

Wealth was becoming increasingly important to the English Church. Grants of land, once clinched by placing a sod of earth on the altar, were now conveyed by written charters, laying down conditions and privileges. Such 'bookland' was frequently freed from taxes to the kingdom and the requirement to provide labour and military service. One responsibility which could not be avoided was the maintenance of defences and bridges. Owners could often bequeath this land as they wished, free from the claims of their kindred. The Church could thus replace the family. Such charters had a significant impact on the national revenue and the king's ability to defend the country. The immunities they granted made forgery a temptation in succeeding centuries.

Bishops of Wilfrid's type needed significant revenues to maintain their courts and build their churches. Benedict's scholarship, too, required a vast expenditure for travel and the purchase of artistic and literary treasures. It is easy to see why Wilfrid would resist the division into smaller bishoprics. Yet it is too simple to dismiss him as corrupted by wealth. He was personally ascetic. In Rome and Lyon he had seen a different vision from the warrior Lord with his personal following or the Anglo-Celtic exemplar of the Servant of the poor. He saw the Church as an empire, with Christ enthroned in majesty, governing through a hierarchy of princely representatives. Dishonour to Bishop Wilfrid was dishonour to God.

7

Early Monasteries, Writing and Art

MONASTERIES

Celtic monasticism often went to extremes of prayer, penance and fasting. In the fifth century, a different model evolved in continental Europe, epitomized by Benedict of Nursia. His Rule was moderate and humane, making allowances for the frailty of human nature, physical and spiritual. He encouraged stability, rather than the Celtic pilgrim vision. There was greater emphasis on corporate worship than on personal experience. Benedictines shared a dormitory, while Celtic monasteries preferred huts for one or two. Wilfrid was proud of having introduced the Benedictine Rule in his monasteries. Benedict Biscop drew on it for his Rule at Wearmouth and Jarrow.

English women enthusiastically took up the monastic career. Women were as ready to give their all for their Lord as their kinsmen were to follow an earthly lord into battle. Monasteries offered new opportunities for young women and security for widows.

Double houses were all headed by an abbess. They included some of the most famous abbeys: Whitby, Ely, Bardney. The degree of segregation varied. At Wimborne, the only man allowed on the women's side was the priest who administered the sacrament and he was not encouraged to linger. When plague struck the monks at Barking, the nuns came out at night to pray over their brothers' graves. Yet elsewhere, men and women sang antiphonally in the choir. Hild and Aelffled attended synods and expressed their opinions forcibly. Cuthbert dined with the nuns of his diocese. Stories that say he banned women from his churches are a later invention.

Sometimes, whole families of women dedicated themselves to this career, like the four daughters of King Anna of East

Anglia. Aethelthryth was the virgin queen of Northumbria and foundress of Ely. Seaxburg was the widow of King Eorconbert of Kent, first abbess on the Isle of Sheppey, then successor to her sister at Ely. Aethelberg was abbess of Brie in Gaul and Witburg a recluse at Dereham. Seaxburg's daughters followed the same vocation.

Her niece Domneva married a Shropshire king. Domneva's two young brothers were murdered by agents of her cousin Egbert, the new king of Kent. When their bodies were discovered buried in the palace, the penitent king offered her land on the island of Thanet for a monastery. Domneva returned to Kent with two of her daughters. Legend says she had a pet hind which ran before her when she was out riding. She let the hind loose on Thanet and claimed the land it covered in a day.

Domneva's eldest daughter Mildburg founded a double house at Much Wenlock with the help of a French nun. Unusually, she became an English saint loved by the Welsh, who knew her from visits she made to her estates there. Another daughter, Mildred, was sent to train at Chelles. Chelles was influenced by the Rule of Columban, an Irish missionary to Europe. Its abbess helped several English monasteries get started. Mildred became abbess of Minster-on-Thanet and one of Kent's favourite saints. Their sister Mildgith remained a simple nun.

Traditional Anglo-Saxon society respected women as a source of wisdom. These nuns had a platform from which to influence policy, national and local, and alleviate poverty, ignorance and ill-health. Some were peasants or former slaves, working at menial tasks. Others studied, taught, preached, wrote, commissioned buildings, copied and painted manuscripts, sang, played and composed music, and travelled as pilgrims and missionaries. Above all, they worshipped God.

Osthryth, daughter of Oswy of Northumbria, married a Mercian king. She wished to transfer the remains of her martyred uncle Oswald Bright-Arm to her favourite monastery of Bardney in Lindsey. But when the monks saw the wagon approaching they shut the gates. Oswald might be a saint, but he was an outsider, who had ruled Lindsey by conquest. The corpse's escort halted and erected an awning over the cart. During the night, a pillar of light is said to have shone skywards from the wagon. The Bardney monks and nuns bowed humbly and brought him into their house. They washed and reinterred Oswald's bones in a splendid tomb and hung his banner of purple and gold over it. The water in which the body was washed proved to have healing powers.

They were slow to realize the potential of a saint's body in a church. Relics became immensely important. They brought an aura of sacredness, attracting pilgrims and devout benefactors. In the eleventh century, Mildred's remains were kidnapped by archiepiscopal body-snatchers.

ALDHELM

In the mid-seventh century, a West Saxon lad, Aldhelm, came to Maildubh's school at Malmesbury in Selwood Forest. He was taught in the Irish tradition. Writers in westernmost Europe had developed a distinctive style of Latin. It was flamboyant, convoluted prose, rich in alliteration and rejoicing in exotic words, bizarrely used. Aldhelm popularized this style. He made friends with an equally enthusiastic fellow student, the future King Aldfrith the Wise of Northumbria.

Aldhelm chose the monastic life in preference to a nobleman's warrior career. In 671 he heard of Theodore and Hadrian's arrival and their revitalization of Canterbury's school with Greek learning. He set out to find what more they could teach him. He wrote back in despair to friends in Wessex. There is so much to learn, so little time. He would love to spend Christmas at Malmesbury, but he has law, literature, music, arithmetic, astronomy, all whirling around in his head. Only illness forced him back to Malmesbury.

He wrote many letters. A friend announced his intention of studying in Ireland. Aldhelm warned him of the dangers. In Irish monasteries, he would be exposed to pagan learning, poetry and legends. He should stick to the pure waters of holy scriptures and shun these muddy pools, with their guttural toads. In another letter he described Theodore savaging Irish students like an angry boar rounding on grinning hounds. But

Maildubh's Irish influence showed in Aldhelm's habit of plunging into a spring for prayer. He stood up to his neck in water, summer or winter, chanting the psalms so beloved by the Celtic Church.

Around 675, Aldhelm succeeded Maildubh as abbot. He replaced the wooden chapel with a finer church and composed a poem for its consecration. Like Aldfrith of Northumbria, he was a poet in Anglo-Saxon as well as Latin. The country people would come to his church for mass, but used to start for home before the sermon. Aldhelm outmanoeuvred them. When they reached the river, he was already standing on the bridge. He sang his entertaining songs until a crowd had gathered, then switched to psalms. They began staying for his sermons.

Aldhelm's correspondence with Aldfrith the Wise illustrated metrical composition with the Anglo-Saxon passion for riddles. He was a keen observer of animal behaviour, both in the Bible and in Selwood Forest. He saw a beaver gnawing a trunk, heard hornets buzzing in a hollow tree, smelt heady elder blossom.

He wrote to seven nuns at Barking, including Cuthburg, sister of King Ine of Wessex and formerly queen of Aldfrith the Wise. After producing a family, the pair had agreed amicably to lead separate, celibate lives. In his treatise, Aldhelm delights in the vigour with which these women pursue their studies, like trained athletes. He extols virginity, male and female. But, conscious of the different sexual experiences of his audience, he warns the true virgins not to be smug, like some lofty lighthouse shining down on lower vessels. There is more humble piety in those who beat between rocks and whirlpools, with Christ as their pilot, and reach haven battered but afloat, than in those who sail only through the calm waters of the monastery with their life-rafts intact. But Aldhelm's true priorities are clear. Virginity equals riches, chastity a modest income, conjugality is poverty. This treatise became one of the most-read works in England.

He offers the nuns tales of rousing heroines, not pious victims. The formidable Victoria is left to die, where a dragon is killing off a whole town. Without weapons or armour, she sees off the dragon, converts the town, and takes up residence in the dragon's lair.

Aldhelm is appalled by the vanity of other monks, nuns and clergy. What are they doing with embroidered silk sleeves, shoes trimmed with red leather, crimping their hair with tongs, sewing ankle-length ribbons on bright headdresses, filing their nails into talons? Wear undyed wool. God did not create sheep scarlet or purple.

An English synod commissioned Aldhelm to write to Geraint, British king of the fast-shrinking Dumnonia. Aldhelm rebukes him for the scandal of disunity with the Roman Church. The Celtic tonsure derives from Simon the Magician, whom Peter cursed. Celtic Easter can mean celebrating on the same day as the Jews. The Welsh will not even pray with the English. They throw food the English have left to dogs and pigs and scour the dishes with sand and ashes. They refuse them the kiss of peace or even water to wash their hands and feet.

When Theodore divided the huge see of Winchester in 705, Aldhelm became first bishop of Sherborne, west of Selwood Forest. He pleaded his advanced age, but was told that his wisdom and experience were just what was needed. He resigned the abbacy of Malmesbury and its daughter houses. But his monks would not hear of losing him and he agreed to combine this workload. He had care of Dorset, Somerset and east Devon. In addition, he had a missionary brief over the British in the far south-west. He narrowly escaped death when a gale flattened a Cornish monastery, sparing only the church where he was conducting the night prayers.

Aldhelm died in 709. His body was carried 50 miles back to Malmesbury, followed by a procession of mourners. Every seven miles they rested, and crosses known as 'bishop-stones' were erected there as memorials.

WEARMOUTH AND JARROW

Benedict Biscop's deputy at Wearmouth was his cousin Eoster-wine, who had been chosen for merit, not nepotism. Like Benedict, Eosterwine exchanged an army career for spiritual battle. He had been a cabinet minister. He started at the bottom at Wearmouth. As deputy abbot, he demonstrated his leadership skills. When he made inspection rounds, he would join in the heaviest work, steering the plough, wielding the blacksmith's hammer, winnowing chaff.

Both Wilfrid and Hild bequeathed their abbeys to kinsfolk. But Benedict obtained from the pope the right of his monks to choose their own abbot. He told them on his deathbed that he would rather his monasteries reverted to wilderness than that his brother, whom he deemed unfit, should inherit.

Ceolfrith, the man they chose, had been Benedict's deputy at Jarrow when plague struck in its first year. Only two people were left who could sing the Latin worship antiphonally: Ceolfrith and a 13-year-old boy, almost certainly Bede. Ceolfrith resorted to reciting the services. But soon he could stand it no longer. He decided that he and the boy would sing the entire three-hourly cycle of daily services between them. It is not surprising that Bede grew up to write two books on the computation of time.

Ceolfrith had been baker at the abbey of Icanhoe in Suffolk before coming to Wearmouth. During one of Benedict's absences, he had so much trouble with an awkward squad of nobly born monks that he packed his satchel and left, preferring sieving flour and cleaning ovens. Benedict fetched him back.

Now, the monks voted him their choice to head the twin monasteries. Ceolfrith's greatest artistic contribution was to commission three mighty volumes, each containing the entire Bible. The Bible was usually bound as separate books, since handwritten volumes were necessarily large, and those displayed on altars particularly so. Up to 1,550 calves would be needed to produce the vellum for just one of Ceolfrith's Bibles, evidence of Wearmouth's wealth.

Ceolfrith feared that, with age, he was again losing his grip on spiritual leadership. He decided to resign and make a final pilgrimage to Rome, taking one of those magnificent Bibles as a present to the pope. He organized a party of 80 monks, but waited till the last moment to tell his monks he was accompanying them. He stood on the chancel steps, giving each the kiss of peace, until mutual grief forced him to stop. They knelt in tears on the beach as he boarded the ferry. Deacons with lighted candles and a golden cross accompanied him across the river.

Ceolfrith did not reach Rome. Local people in Burgundy attended his funeral, grieving for this stranger who had not been able to fulfil his last wish. The gift of English scribes and artists he was carrying is the world's oldest complete Latin Bible still in existence.

BEDE

In 680, a boy of seven was given to Wearmouth. Five years later he accompanied Ceolfrith the few miles north to begin a new community at Jarrow. He never left this area. Yet his learning spanned the earth and heavens. Without him, it would not be possible to tell a coherent story of the early English Church.

Worship is the principal business of a monastery. Time regulated its services. Festivals and fasts required lunar and solar calendars. Bede wrote two books on the nature of time, beginning from creation. He popularized the calculation of dates from the Incarnation instead of a king's reign.

He contributed a metrical and a prose *Life of Cuthbert*, *Lives* of the early abbots of Wearmouth and Jarrow, biblical commentaries and a monumental *History of the English Church and People*. He is a remarkably conscientious historian, identifying his sources and distinguishing first-hand from second-hand information. Northumbrian history dominates, but he requested information from other kingdoms. Some supplied him with colourful tales, others dry lists of facts. One informant went to Rome to find Gregory's letters. Bede wove it all into a saga that had meaning and purpose: the winning of the English people for Christ. For all its scholarship, it was not written to inform, but to change people.

The story focuses on kings and clergy, monks and hermits. We learn practically nothing about lay people, unless they are royal or the recipients of miraculous healing. But there are far-reaching implications in his title, 'the English Church and

People'. Warring kingdoms have a shared origin and destiny, under one God.

In 734, near the end of Bede's life, his friend Egbert was appointed bishop of York. Bede wrote him a passionate letter, lamenting the state of the church in Northumbria. The hill farms and hamlets in remote dales have not seen their bishop for years. Yet they have to pay tax to him. The lure of money encourages men to take on wider responsibilities than they can possibly discharge. Bede urges Egbert to carry out Pope Gregory's original intention and consecrate 12 bishops for the north, with priests and teachers in every village. Everyone should know the Lord's Prayer and the Apostles' Creed, in English if necessary.

He warns of the uncontrolled rash of independent monasteries. The economic balance is shifting from Crown to Church. There are no longer the funds to maintain a proper army. Some are monasteries in name only, where bogus monks live a life of luxury and escape military service and taxes. Egbert must dissolve them and use the revenue for more bishops.

Bede died that same year at Jarrow. Early in the morning he started dictating his translation of John's Gospel and the scholar Isidore into Anglo-Saxon. He was having trouble breathing. The bell rang for a Rogationtide procession around the fields. One novice stayed behind. 'There's still one chapter left,' he said, 'but it seems hard for you to keep answering questions.' 'No,' said Bede. 'Sharpen your pen and write fast.' In the afternoon he suddenly called his brother priests. He distributed his meagre possessions: pepper, napkins, incense. Then he sent them away and dictated the last sentence. He died with his head cradled on the boy's arm.

GUTHLAC OF CROWLAND

Guthlac never imagined that he would end his life as a hermit in the Anglian fens. He was born in 674, to noble parents in eastern Mercia. Everyone assumed he would become a warrior and he was brought up on the stirring lays of heroes. At 15, he entered military service.

His career took him to the turbulent border with the Welsh.

For the next nine years, Guthlac sacked and pillaged their towns, farms and fortresses. There are hints that he suffered a traumatic experience, captured by the British. He learned their language. At the age of 24, it struck Guthlac that the hero stories he had revelled in as a boy ended in wretched deaths, riches lost, glory forgotten. He stared his own death in the face.

He told his warband to find themselves another leader and took himself to the abbess of Repton. Where once he had dreamed of becoming a hero with a sword, now he longed for the heroism of the hermit. After two years, the abbess let him try.

Guthlac chose the fenland, 90 miles away. It was a sinister wasteland of rivers, black bogs and wind in the reeds. A fisherman rowed him out north of Cambridge to the uninhabited island of Crowland. Guthlac was delighted and returned from Repton with two boys to help him. He chose for his hermitage an ancient barrow and built his turf hut over the dug-out base. He wore animal skins and ate only after sunset, just barley bread and muddy water.

He found that the contemplative life held perils as frightening as that of the warrior. He was soon overwhelmed with despair at the impossibility of what he had undertaken. After three days and nights of intense depression, he was comforted by a vision of the martyred apostle Bartholomew.

Demons tempted him to fast six days a week. Guthlac promptly ate the scrap of bread he had been saving for the evening.

At the dead of night, the haunting came back, worse than ever. Devils were coming at him from every corner of the hut, up through the floor, wriggling through the wattle walls. They were grotesquely ugly, with huge heads, yellow faces, horses' teeth, knotted knees. They vomited flames and screeched raucously. They bound him, dragged him outside, plunged him into scummy swamps, pulled him through brambles, beat him with iron rods. When Guthlac stood firm, they whisked him up into the winter storm clouds. He saw sulphurous flames, icy hail, the gate of hell. St Bartholomew ordered the evil spirits to take him home. As the sun rose, he found two of them weeping, their power broken.

On another occasion, his nightmares took a terrifyingly recognizable form. He heard the roar of a mob around his hut, the voices of British soldiers on the roof. He rushed outside, fearing the settlement was about to go up in flames. The enemy Britons hoisted him on the points of their spears. Only his shout of the psalm, 'Let God arise!' sent them vanishing like smoke.

They returned in the form of dangerous animals. Such dark, demonic visions of the presence of evil haunted the Anglo-Saxon imagination for centuries.

Yet, amid these psychological and physical dangers, Guthlac preserved his sense of humour. His friend Wilfrid was devastated when a jackdaw stole his unfinished manuscript. Guthlac grabbed a skiff and made him row after it. They found the manuscript balanced on a bent reed, the precious pages only a hairsbreadth from the water. When the jackdaws stole Wilfrid's gloves, Guthlac teased him for his disproportionate grief. Wilfrid had to climb on the roof to retrieve one. Guthlac was holding the other in his hand, grinning.

Guthlac was a layman. He only spent two years in a monastery. But his spiritual and physical healing was sought by the poor and the sick, abbots and nobles, even by an exiled prince who later became king of Mercia. The bishop of Lichfield's librarian was suspicious of hermits, fearing them tainted with Celtic schism. Guthlac passed his test. The bishop consecrated his church on Crowland Island and ordained Guthlac priest.

SAINTS' LIVES

A *Life of Saint Anthony* inspired a spate of English imitators. One of the first was written by a Whitby monk. It is the earliest account ever compiled of the life of Gregory the Great. Gregory was revered at Whitby as the man who sent Augustine to convert Abbess Aelffled's great-grandfather, King Aethelbert of Kent.

The love for Cuthbert gave rise to *Lives*, one written on Lindisfarne and two by Bede. A loyal *Life of Wilfrid* was written by his choirmaster Eddi. It was not used much outside

Wilfrid's monasteries. Others written soon after their subjects died were Felix's *Life of Saint Guthlac of Crowland* and the *Life* of the Irish hermit Fursey of East Anglia. An exception to these ecclesiastics is the *Life of Oswald*, the king who founded Lindisfarne. Guthlac's story, too, seems aimed at a lay audience.

A necessary element in these stories is the miracles attributed to saints, in their lifetime or after. The author of Gregory's *Life* is new to the game. He apologizes for the lack of miracles associated with Gregory, though he then goes on to recount a remarkable posthumous appearance, in which the former pope kicks in the head of an unbeliever. Others simply copied what they had read elsewhere. Eddi's description of Wilfrid's character is taken word for word from the Lindisfarne *Life of Cuthbert*, though it would be difficult to imagine two contemporary characters more unlike. But the Lindisfarne eulogy itself is not original. Reginald of Durham, writing in Norman times, justifies this as 'the communion of saints'. 'If I came across a good story anywhere, I put it in. Even if my man didn't do it, some other saint did.' It is as well not to take anything as incontrovertible fact. The details most likely to be true are those which occur nowhere else. The infant who foretells that Cuthbert will grow up to be a bishop provokes a yawn. The information that at the time Cuthbert was standing on his head showing his bare bottom makes us sit up and hope this may be genuine.

These early writers gilded the haloes of their subjects. The tendency of our own time is to reveal the feet of clay. All biographers have their own agenda. The intention of a saint's *Life* was to lead its audience closer to heaven. Miracle stories are not simply evidence of credulity. They enflesh the view that the whole of life is lived in the dimension of the divine.

CROSSES

In the conversion era, a standing cross was often the focus for Christian worship before a church could be built. At first they were wooden, but by the eighth century magnificent stone examples were appearing. One huge cross of Northumbrian workmanship stands now in the chancel of Ruthwell kirk in

Dumfriesshire. It is six metres tall. There is a wealth of decorative and pictorial carving. It also carries runic inscriptions, unusual in Christian art. They include lines from the great Anglo-Saxon poem, 'The Dream of the Rood'. Ceolfrith of Wearmouth and Jarrow was in Rome in 701 when the pope discovered a piece of wood believed to be part of Christ's cross. Veneration of the cross became a powerful element in Anglo-Saxon spirituality.

Crosses of this period are not crucifixes. Christ appears robed in majesty, resurrected. Christ is the heroic lord, leading his warband to victory. He is also a priest-king, ruling in glory.

POETRY

Two Anglo-Saxon enthusiasms, the riddle and the veneration of the cross, come together brilliantly in 'The Dream of the Rood'. It touches, too, on pre-Christian reverence for the World Tree. The poet sees the cross as a 'glory-tree' shining with gold and gems, surrounded by adoring angels. Yet it shimmers with blood and sweat. The 'Healer's Tree' speaks. It was felled and fashioned into a scaffold. It saw the young hero coming to mount it and struggled to stay upright. 'I raised the great King, liege lord of the heavens.' Nails wounded them both. Strange wyrds surrounded them, darkness fell. Earls took Christ down and uttered the grief-song. The three weeping crosses were cut down and buried in a pit. Then the 'Lord's men' found the true cross and decked it with jewels.

The poem 'Elene' tells of the emperor Constantine's mother Helena discovering Christ's cross.

'Andreas' celebrates Andrew, the missionary apostle. The Anglo-Saxons were famous seafarers. Andrew's voyages become a saga of longships. Christ is the 'Wave's Warden', master of his vessel. The apostles are 'twelve mighty heroes', 'thanes of God', battling with shield and helmet in a clash of banners.

The ninth-century poem 'Genesis' inspired Milton's 'Paradise Lost'. Lucifer rejects his Lord. He has loyal companions and can raise his own throne higher. Like an Anglo-Saxon warleader, he reminds his fallen followers of the treasures with which he once rewarded them.

The workforce of the monasteries enabled a blossoming of books, copies of existing works and original compositions. They were not all beautifully written and ornamented. The missionary Boniface complained of tiny letters and abbreviations. The reverence with which we now view handwritten manuscripts, under glass in air-conditioned rooms, disguises the reality. The Anglo-Saxons treated their books as an international lending library. If a friend requested it, texts were sent around the English kingdoms, or to mission outposts across the Rhine.

The great illuminated Gospels were for liturgical use. They were placed on the altar as sacred works of art, the Word of God made visible.

The greatest gem that survives is the Lindisfarne Gospels. We have the names of its makers: Eadfrith the scribe, bishop of Lindisfarne from 698, Aethelwald who bound it, and the anchorite Billfrith who adorned it with gold, silver and gems. In the tenth century, the priest Aldred inserted an Old English translation between the Latin lines.

There are carpet pages, dense with ornament, whole page depictions of each evangelist, astonishing initial letters from which animal heads emerge. Ribbons of colour weave through the design or spin within circles. The Anglo-Saxon design is more angular and symmetrical than its Celtic contemporaries, like the *Book of Kells*, yet it displays the same exuberance of imagination in the convoluted bodies, the ability to surprise. The evangelists are depicted in the Italian style, as human beings, with their symbols of man, lion, bull or eagle hovering overhead. Another haloed head, possibly Christ, peeps round a curtain as St Matthew writes. Despite the controlled design, there are small discrepancies: one bird with striped wings when the rest are uniformly feathered, a detail left unfinished. Perfection in creation is only for God.

CHURCH FURNISHINGS

Time has preserved little of the ecclesiastical embroidery for which Englishwomen were famous. A fragment of a stole placed in Cuthbert's coffin later shows the head of John the Baptist. The altar at Hexham was hung with purple silk. When Aldhelm celebrated mass in the pope's church in Rome he wore a chasuble of red silk embroidered with peacocks.

Aldhelm brought back from Rome a papal gift of a white marble altar. It cracked in two when the donkey bearing it collapsed on an Alpine path. Wilfrid and Benedict Biscop returned from the continent with paintings to hang in their churches.

Aldhelm wrote a poem celebrating the dedication of Abbess Bugga's church at Withington, near Cirencester, in 690. She had glass in the windows, diffusing sunshine through the 'four-square' building, an altar resplendent with a brilliantly jewelled chalice and gold, silver and gems on its splendid cross.

CHURCH BUILDINGS

Early churches were small. As numbers in an abbey grew, more oratories were added. Augustine's mission recycled Roman brick. Stone churches followed the tradition of timbered halls, tall narrow buildings with a raftered roof. But Hexham had one circular church like a Byzantine basilica.

Stone benches around an apse would enable clergy to sit facing the congregation. The chief celebrant occupied a central 'frith stool', or 'peace seat'.

At Canterbury's abbey church the royal family and bishops were buried in side chambers around the nave. By the late eighth century, St Peter's in York had become a splendid building surrounded by side chapels, with 30 altars. The later Anglo-Saxons developed a fondness for upstairs chapels, which may still be detected by high sculptures or windows.

Anglo-Saxon imagination ornamented the plain architecture. There were decorative friezes, carved porches, ornamented pillars. Birds and beasts feeding on grapes were a typical motif. Christ is the vine who nourishes us.

Christian art conveyed the gospel to a largely illiterate people. The growing wealth of the Church enabled artistic patronage. Poetry sings in the heart. Gospels in gold on purple vellum, supplied by the abbess of Thanet, Mary Magdalene washing Christ's feet with her tears on the Ruthwell Cross, speak at a more profound level than prose.

8

The English and Europe

WILLIBRORD

Missionary campaigns required the consent of kings. Most
people followed their lord's lead. Such mass conversions
were shallow and many continued to propitiate their old
gods.

Wilfrid had carried out a short missionary campaign in
Frisia, whose language was closest to English. Another
Northumbrian, Willibrord from Humberside, stayed till he
died. Unlike many Church leaders, he was not a nobleman.
His parents dedicated him to Christ at the foot of the local
standing cross. Later, his father left the family to found his own
monastery on Spurn Point. Willibrord was given to Wilfrid's
monastery school at Ripon. At the age of 20, he went to study
in Ireland. Here he made friends with two English monks,
Egbert and Witbert.

Egbert had planned to evangelize the Germans, with whom
the English felt a kinship. He had got together an expedition
for the purpose when an outbreak of plague changed his life.
He determined to devote his energies to church unity among
the Celts.

Egbert's friend Witbert actually got as far as Frisia. But the
king who had welcomed Wilfrid was dead. His heathen son
Radbod had no time for Christianity. After two years of frus-
tration, Witbert returned to Ireland.

Willibrord spent 12 years listening to the tales of these
would-be missionaries, until the call of Frisia became
inescapable. With 11 companions he sailed up the Rhine to
Utrecht. King Radbod blocked his plans. There is a story that
Radbod was temporarily converted by a visiting Frankish bishop.
He got as far as the baptistry and was dipping his foot in the

water when he asked, 'Where will I find more of my royal ancestors; in heaven or hell?' Receiving the standard answer of those times, that the unbaptized are damned, he chose to spend eternity with his kin. He wrecked Frankish churches in his lands.

Willibrord switched to an alternative plan. The Frankish ruler Pippin had captured some Frisian land. Pippin was a devout Christian and happy to give Willibrord entry. Willibrord set a precedent for English missionaries by going to Rome to ask papal authority for his work. A stream of English men and women came out to help him in Utrecht. Hewald the White and Hewald the Black pressed on to the border with the Old Saxons. They were murdered and their bodies dumped in the Rhine.

Willibrord's elevation to archbishop of the Frisians was Pippin's idea. He saw himself becoming ruler of the same larger territory. He gave Willibrord land, wealth, workers, and Utrecht castle for his archbishop's palace. Churches and monasteries were built at Utrecht and Echternach and across the countryside. But the hostile King Radbod still held much of Frisia.

Willibrord turned his energies to Denmark, but left disappointed. He did, however, bring back 30 Danish boys. He began instructing them as soon as the journey started, fearing they might drown or die in an ambush before he could baptize them. He was right to be anxious. A storm drove them on to Heligoland – Holy Island. In those days it was called Fositeland, after a local god. There was a sacred spring, with a taboo on speaking near it, and sacred cows grazing. Willibrord baptized three converts in the spring and ordered some cattle to be killed to provide food. The horrified local people reported him to King Radbod, who declared the god must be propitiated with human blood. Lots were cast, three times a day for three days. One of Willibrord's party was singled out, and went to martyrdom bravely. The rest were allowed to return to Utrecht.

In 714, Pippin died and King Radbod snatched back his conquered territory. He wrecked Willibrord's mission churches. The English retreated to Echternach.

At this critical moment, another Englishman arrived.

The man we know as Boniface began life as Wynfrith. He was born around 675 in east Devon, recently captured by the West Saxons. His own decision to enter a monastery as a small child was inspired by missionaries visiting the house. In vain, his family tried to talk, beat, or bribe him out of it. At last his father conceded that his son's vocation was genuine and handed him over to the abbot of Exeter.

Wynfrith moved on to Nursling to improve his education. He showed a gift for teaching and was willing to learn from his pupils as well as instruct them. Women as well as men attended his lectures and he taught some by correspondence. He represented his bishop at a national synod and won respect.

He stunned his community when, in 716, he announced his wish to throw up a promising ecclesiastical career and become a missionary. But they rallied, and sent him on his way generously supplied, with some volunteer companions and a mutual promise of prayer.

They landed near Utrecht, now on the wrong side of the battle line. Pippin's illegitimate son Charles Martel, or 'the Hammer', had declared himself mayor of Austrasia, kingdom of the eastern Franks. He was fighting King Radbod. Radbod wanted nothing to do with Christian missionaries. Wynfrith's party returned to Nursling.

After two years, he was impatient to try again. The brothers wanted Wynfrith to become their next abbot, but his bishop released him. Like Willibrord, he journeyed to Rome to gain the pope's authority for his mission. The pope smiled at his enthusiasm and gave him a new name, Boniface.

The territory assigned to him was Thuringia, in the Harz mountains. Boniface was on his way to gain secular authority from Charles the Hammer when he learned that King Radbod had died. The way was again open for mission in Frisia.

Willibrord returned to his cathedral in Utrecht and resumed work. The battle between Christians and heathens took physical form. When Willibrord smashed the statue of a pre-Christian deity, the infuriated custodian attacked him with a sword, aiming at his head. The bishop's companions fell on the man. Willibrord intervened to save him, but he died shortly afterwards.

Boniface diverted his route down the Rhine to offer his services. He helped the ageing archbishop restore the shattered mission, rebuilding churches.

BONIFACE IN GERMANY

Boniface refused Willibrord's request to take on the archbishopric of Frisia. Hesse, east of the Rhine, was now under Frankish rule. The Frankish Church was little interested in missionary work, but Irish missionaries had been there.

Again Boniface reported to the pope. There is something comical about his encounter in 722 with Gregory II. The Devonian and the Italian could not understand each other's Latin. Boniface had to write out his answers to the pope's questions on his beliefs and adherence to Catholic doctrine. He satisfied the pontiff, and was made a bishop. Boniface was an Englishman, not bound to the Roman Empire. There were two departures from the normal bishop's oath of allegiance to the Church. Boniface was not required to vow loyalty to the Emperor in Constantinople. But he must swear to oppose bishops not in conformity with the Roman Church and report them to the pope. The Roman Church still feared Irish missionaries, whose continental foundations preserved some of their past autonomous spirit. As a loyal companion of his lord, Boniface remained true to that oath, sworn over the tomb of St Peter.

Conditions for the sort of men he might not ordain jar on the modern ear. No one who was maimed was eligible. Nor was an African. North Africans were suspected of heresy and undergoing a second baptism.

For the rest of his life, Boniface maintained a hotline to the pope, frequently reporting in person. He even wrote to ask the pope how long bacon fat should be kept before eating.

Boniface went to Hesse with the backing of Charles and the pope. There was there an ancient oak, sacred to Jupiter, a romanization of the thunder god Thunor. Local Christians urged Boniface to fell it. They still feared its power. Even some Christians apparently sold their slaves for sacrifice. Legend says that, as Boniface swung his axe, a mighty wind blew the tree over. It cracked into four pieces, awing the crowd of furious heathens. With the timber, Boniface built a chapel on the site.

Boniface's old bishop, Daniel of Winchester, wrote him a letter, advising him how to approach heathens. He recommends patient discussion and logical argument.

The pope made Boniface archbishop to the Germans, with his see at Mainz.

BONIFACE'S LETTERS

Busy though he was, Boniface kept up correspondence with friends and admirers in Britain. They sought advice, encouragement, writings, and sent gifts for his churches and books he requested. One abbess wrote in despair of her monastery's bad harvest, of crippling taxes, of the weight of pastoral care of so many men and women. She wishes she could come to Frisia to receive Boniface's comfort in person.

She asks his advice about making a pilgrimage to Rome. We can guess Boniface's answer from his letter to another abbess, Bugga. He does not absolutely forbid pilgrimage. But if she thinks she will gain peace of soul after the stress of managing an institution, then she has underestimated the hazards and problems of the journey. A religious sister in Rome advises that she wait until the threat of Saracen attack has passed. Boniface later writes to the archbishop of Canterbury urging the English Church and monarchs to forbid women, including nuns, to make these frequent journeys to Rome. He says many of them never arrive, and few retain their virtue. In almost every city of Frankland, Lombardy and Gaul, there are English prostitutes. Bugga did make it to Rome and met Boniface there.

WILLIBALD'S TRAVELS

Turning to Bavaria, Boniface complained to the pope that his work was hampered by decadent Frankish Catholics, undisciplined Irish, and obstinate heathens. Could he not go back to

Frisia, now Willibrord had retired to Echternach? The pope said no, but found Boniface another English assistant.

Willibald had set out, with his brother Wynnebald and their reluctant father, on pilgrimage to Rome. The father died on the journey. Willibald left his brother in Rome and set off with companions to wander round the holy sites of the eastern Mediterranean. Twice they were arrested by Saracens on suspicion of spying. In Syria, they were released when a rich old man declared that the English were harmless; they did this sort of thing to fulfil their law. In Jerusalem, a sympathetic merchant sent them dinner and supper in prison every day. On Wednesdays and Saturdays his son was allowed to visit them and take them out for a bath. On Sundays, he escorted them to church, taking them through the market place in case they wanted to do any shopping. Local people peered into their cell at these blond, strangely dressed youngsters. They were finally allowed to go free without even a bribe.

Willibald returned to the Benedictine monastery of Monte Cassino. He was acting as a tour guide in Rome to a Spanish priest when the pope summoned him. He found himself heading for Bavaria to assist Boniface. A year later, he received a message telling him to go to a monastery in Thuringia. To his joy, he found that the abbot was his brother Wynnebald, whom Boniface had also found in Rome.

ARCHBISHOP TO THE GERMANS

Boniface resisted the temptation to retain sole control. He appointed more bishops for Hesse, Thuringia and Bavaria, with Willibald as a roving bishop with a mainly missionary brief.

He continued to battle against Franks, Irish and heathens. He imprisoned an Irish missionary bishop for teaching that Christ descended into hell to free both Christians and heathens. Another Irishman was abbot of Salzburg with a bishop under him, in the old Celtic tradition. Boniface reported him to the pope for maintaining that there are people living under our earth.

He was scandalized by the Frankish clergy. They were

womanizers and drunkards, they hunted and marched to war. He called synods to regularize Christian life. His example was emulated by the English Church.

Boniface and King Aethelbald

Aethelbald, the exiled prince whom Guthlac had comforted, was now the powerful king of Mercia. He attracted Boniface's wrath. Boniface wrote from Germany that the English were gaining a reputation on the continent as a nation of adulterers, and he held the Mercian king responsible.

Boniface was a West Saxon archbishop in Germany. He had never lived in Mercia. Yet he assumed the right to have a say in its government. The pope had given him a mission to the Germanic peoples of Europe. Boniface evidently interpreted that as including Anglo-Saxons, as well as Old Saxons.

Boniface and seven Anglo-Saxon bishops reproved King Aethelbald for not taking a wife, not from chastity, but because he preferred illicit relationships, including the seduction of nuns. Boniface quotes, almost with approval, the Old Saxon custom of forcing an adulteress, single or married, to hang herself, and then hanging her partner over her funeral pyre. Or else a mob of women chase her through the street, whipping and beating her, stripping her to the waist and stabbing her. The whole idea of marriage caused celibate priests considerable anxiety. The rules for it play a large part in the laws they drew up.

Boniface was influential in the calling of an English synod at the unidentified location of Cloveshoe in 747. The archbishop of Canterbury presided. King Aethelbald came too, doubtless to see that his interests were not overridden.

Bishops must tour their dioceses, often huge, once a year. Priests must avoid worldly cares and give their time to reading, prayer and pastoral oversight. They must be trained in the meaning of their offices and sacraments. They should not declaim services like a secular poet. They may not all know Latin, but the intention of the heart makes up for deficiency in intellectual understanding. The laity will despise the clergy for heavy drinking. Rogation days are for solemn processions, not feasts, games and horse races.

Monasteries have fallen into sad decline. Monks and nuns should pray, study and run schools. Both should avoid flamboyant dress. Nuns are not to spend time on elaborate embroidery. A monastery is no place for poets, harpists and clowns.

MISSIONARY NUNS

Wynnebald, Willibald's brother, built a monastery in the forest of Heidenheim. Their sister Walburg, called by the Germans Walpurgis, came over from England to help him run it. After Wynnebald died, Walburg became sole abbess.

She brought a kinswoman. This English nun wrote *Lives* of both Wynnebald and his brother. For centuries, she was known only as 'the Anonymous Nun of Heidenheim'. In the twentieth century it was discovered that she had hidden her name in a cryptogram, bound between her two stories: Huneberc.

Huneberc's approach is refreshing. She retains some of her interviewee's words in the first person. What fascinates her is not Willibald's august career as a bishop, but his youthful pilgrimage. She gives us unique information about the Middle East in the eighth century: stylites living on columns, pilgrims holding a rope across the Jordan as they plunge in, the Church of the Ascension standing open to the sky. Other Christian writers are hostile to the Saracens, at this time of Moorish invasions, but Huneberc tells of their courtesy towards English prisoners. Instead of miracles, she gives us a description of the future bishop's method of smuggling. On leaving Jerusalem, Willibald packed a gourd with fragrant balsam. He plugged the neck with a reed filled with petroleum, to deceive the customs officers who sniffed it. Had he been caught, the penalty was death.

FULDA

A disciple of Boniface, Sturm, penetrated the forests of the Fulda valley, tributary of the Weser. Here, in 744, he built a monastery which became the old archbishop's favourite retreat, like Willibrord's Echternach. While his retinue felled trees for its church, Boniface found a hilltop for solitary prayer. Boniface sent Sturm to Rome and Monte Cassino, to gain a thorough grounding in the Benedictine Rule. Fulda became a fountainhead for scholarship in Frankland and Germany.

Leoba

In 732, Boniface received a letter written by a young kinswoman, known affectionately as Leoba, 'the Beloved'. The fatherless young nun says she looks on Boniface as her brother. She has been studying poetic composition under Boniface's friend Eadburg, abbess of Minster-in-Thanet. Leoba encloses some verses of her own for criticism.

It was said of Leoba that she had a merry face, though she never burst out laughing. She continued her training at Wimborne, where a harsh nun made the lives of the younger ones a misery. Even on her deathbed, she would not ask forgiveness from those she had wronged. The young sisters dutifully attended her funeral. But afterwards, they jumped up and down on her grave so hard that it sank below ground level. The abbess recognized the force of divine justice, but preached them a sharp sermon on Christian forgiveness and ordered three days' fast. When they emerged from church after praying for the deceased, the grave mound was found restored.

Leoba emerged as a considerable scholar, loving biblical studies above all. Around 748 Boniface asked the abbess of Wimborne to send Leoba to head the work among women in Germany. The abbess was not at all pleased to part with her. Leoba came with four other nuns. They set about independently founding schools and monasteries for women. Leoba's own abbey at Tauberbischofsheim trained a new generation of leaders.

Leoba insisted her nuns take a siesta after lunch in summer, in accordance with the Benedictine Rule. She would not allow them to stay up late, even to pray. She scolded the ascetics, 'If you don't rest, you won't be fit to study.' She made sure the food was good, and the hospitality generous, even if she was fasting herself. When she lay down to rest, young nuns took turns at reading the Bible to her. Sometimes, when they thought she was falling asleep, they made deliberate mistakes. But they never caught her out. She always came to and supplied the correct words.

When a terrible storm hit and roofs blew off, the villagers fled to the abbey church and locked themselves in. Leoba flung off her cloak and stood in the doorway, challenging the elements, until the hurricane, thunder and lightning rolled away.

Her knowledge of biblical and patristic writings, canon law and chronology was extensive. Her advice was sought by abbots, bishops and kings. But she hated court life, preferring to tour her monasteries, and chastised the queen for summoning her out of retirement to attend her deathbed.

Towards the end of his life, Boniface summoned Leoba and gave her his cowl. He begged her never to leave her adopted land, even if she felt herself growing weak, but rather to extend her work. He wished to be buried at Fulda and he asked that Leoba be buried alongside him when her time came, so that they might be raised at the resurrection side by side, as they had laboured together in this life.

BONIFACE'S DEATH

Boniface met his end in Frisia, the seaboard that first attracted him. He was traversing its canals and rivers on a missionary campaign, camping with his fellow evangelists. One June morning in 754, he was due to hold a mass confirmation of converts. At sunrise, an armed mob attacked the Christian camp. Boniface seized the holy relics he always carried with him and came out of his tent, calling the others. Some of his escort grabbed up weapons. Boniface ordered them to put them down. 'Scripture tells us to overcome evil with good. They cannot touch our souls.' Boniface and 30 others were murdered.

The assassins seized the party's travelling chests, believing they held treasure. They got drunk on the wine they found on the archbishop's ships and fights broke out. But when they opened the chests, all they found were books. In disgust, they scattered them over the fields, tossing many of them into the marsh. Some were rescued. One damaged Gospel was said to be the one with which Boniface tried to protect his head as he was mown down.

In spite of Boniface's plea, avenging Christians slaughtered the assailants. They took their wives and children into slavery.

There was a squabble over Boniface's body. Mainz and Utrecht both claimed it. But Boniface's wish was honoured and he was buried at Fulda. Women had not been allowed to enter this monastery, but an exception was made so that Leoba could pray at Boniface's tomb. She had to leave the rest of her party at a guesthouse outside, bringing only one older nun to chaperone her. After praying, she conversed with the brothers, but left before nightfall. As Boniface wished, she was herself buried at Fulda in 779. The monks were afraid to open Boniface's tomb to lay her with him, so they interred her beside the altar.

Boniface's legacy of loyalty was the establishment of papal authority across a wide area of Europe. He left an efficient administration, from Rome down to parish priest. National churches, autonomous abbeys, freelance missionaries were all on the way out. This trend was not yet as strong in the English kingdoms. But Boniface created a model which could not be ignored.

The School at York

In 735 Egbert, friend and former pupil of Bede, became the first archbishop of York. He set about founding a cathedral school and became its enlightened first principal. That year, Alcuin was born in York. He came from the same family as Willibrord of Frisia and inherited the Humberside monastery founded by Willibrord's father.

At York, Egbert added secular literature, liberal arts and science to Bede's curriculum. He believed in specialist teachers for each subject. Alcuin studied Virgil, Cicero and Aristotle, as well as biblical scholarship, grammar and rhetoric, astronomy, church law and music, biology and arithmetic. Egbert was an inspirational teacher and pastor. Most mornings, he sat on his bed in his cell and anyone could come and ask him questions or have their arguments challenged by his keen mind. No pupil went to bed without Egbert's hand laid in blessing on his head.

Aelbert, another great teacher, took over the school. He made frequent visits to the continent to acquire fresh texts. Aelbert took Alcuin with him to Rome, to Pavia, the capital of Lombardy, and to Frankland. The reputation of York's school spread. When Aelbert became archbishop, Alcuin took over the school.

Alcuin chose not to become a monk or a priest, though he lived communally with the minster clergy. He remained a deacon all his life, finding his true vocation in teaching. He wrote passionately about education. Without teachers, salvation is impossible. Feeding the hungry soul is even more important than giving bread to the poor.

ALCUIN AND CHARLEMAGNE

Charlemagne, or Charles the Great, was king of the Franks and much of the Germanic lands and grandson of Boniface's patron, Charles the Hammer. He was an enthusiastic patron of learning and a lifelong student. In 781, Alcuin was returning from Rome after collecting the new archbishop's *pallium*. He stopped at Parma, where he was headhunted by Charlemagne for the post of master of his palace school in Aachen. Alcuin was at first reluctant, but became convinced that education was the key to converting the Franks and Germans.

It was an intellectually exciting atmosphere. A colleague complained it was like living in a hurricane. Charlemagne wanted to restore the educational riches of Europe. King, queen, princes and princesses, family, friends, and visitors, all were swept into the palace school, as well as formal students. Alcuin remembered one of the young princesses slipping out at night to watch the stars and how her thoughts moved from astronomy to worshipping the creator of this beauty.

Alcuin gave every pupil an affectionate nickname. Charlemagne was 'King David'. Alcuin's own nickname was 'Flabby'. He continued to correspond with pupils after they left. He laments that, in youth's springtime, 'Cuckoo' has flown the place of religion and learning. Will he come back when the cowslips are budding again? Another colleague writes an affectionate poem, describing how Father Alcuin bursts from theological discussion into lyric poetry or teasing riddles. But his diet of porridge and cheese is too frugal; he needs more wine and meat to make him really good company.

The king wanted a standard liturgy throughout his realm. Alcuin produced a Sacramentary, but added a supplement in which he gathered, 'like spring flowers from the meadows', prayers for special occasions and the Frankish saints beloved by the people. Alcuin was not an original thinker. What the two of them achieved was to raise the standard of teaching throughout Charlemagne's great kingdom.

THE CONVERSION OF SAXONY

Willehad came from the same Northumbrian family as Willibrord and Alcuin, the last of the vigorous line of eighth-century English missionaries in Europe. He arrived around 770 to work among the Frisians.

Beyond, between the Weser and the Elbe, lay the Old Saxons, still resolutely heathen. The English regarded Saxons as their kin and longed to convert them. Charlemagne saw conversion as a political tool, as well as a spiritual blessing. He sent his troops in and ordered the Saxons to accept Christ at the point of the sword. We begin to see the concept of a 'holy war': not self-defence against heathen attack, but conquest justified as salvation. In 780, Charlemagne sent Willehad to be spiritual leader of this reluctant flock.

Charlemagne's Christianizing policy was repressive. It was a capital offence to refuse baptism, to eat meat during Lent, or to persist in the Saxon custom of cremating the dead. The Saxons rose in vengeance and massacred the incomers, including priests, nuns and monks. Willehad escaped to Echternach. Charlemagne is said to have beheaded 4,500 captives in revenge. Three years later, the nationalist Saxon leader accepted baptism, with Charlemagne as his godfather. It was a political, as well as a religious, submission. Pope Hadrian wrote to

Charlemagne praising the divine mercy that 'the heathens have come under your royal rule into the true religion and perfect faith'. Willehad resumed work as bishop of Bremen.

Alcuin was loyal to both king and pope, but he had his sticking-point. At first he was as exultant as anyone at the conversion of the 'unspeakable Saxons'. Doubt slowly surfaces. 'You can drive someone to baptism, but not to faith.' When Charlemagne's 'Christian army' used the same methods against the Avars of Hungary, Alcuin begged him to show mercy and use discretion in converting them to Christianity.

A western Holy Roman Empire and western Church were in the making. In 726, the emperor in Constantinople, influenced by a convert to Islam, had forbidden all figurative religious art. In 787 the Greek-born empress Irene persuaded an ecumenical council to allow the veneration of images, but not their worship. Both Alcuin and Charlemagne misunderstood this edict, which was badly translated into Latin. They believed it required Christians to adore images. Alcuin led English and Frankish condemnation. In 795, the newly elected Pope Leo III sent the keys of the shrine of St Peter and the standard of Rome not to Constantinople but to Charlemagne, offering him Rome's oath of homage. The English Church was friend to Charlemagne and loyal to the pope.

OFFA OF MERCIA

But there had been doubts about that loyalty. Aethelbald of Mercia was murdered by his bodyguards and succeeded by Offa, whom some styled 'King of the English'. Mercia was in the ascendent. There were rumours that Offa had proposed to Charlemagne that they depose Pope Hadrian I and have a new pope elected. Hadrian tactfully says that he does not believe the rumour. But in 786 papal legates arrived, the only such delegation to Britain in Anglo-Saxon times. They proceeded on a tour of inspection.

The result was a synod in Northumbria, whose decisions were also ratified by Canterbury. Bishops must only ordain suitable people. The priest must say the daily offices publicly, and wear proper vestments, not showing his bare legs. There should be decent communion bread for the people, not crusts and crumbs. An order of secular, or non-monastic, cathedral canons is recognized. They should live communally, obeying their rule, and not eat on their own, unless ill.

It is the duty of godparents to teach their charges the Lord's Prayer and the Creed. Only births within marriage are recognized as legitimate. Natural children are not eligible to inherit property or to become priests or kings. This ruling would have excluded Aldfrith the Wise.

For the first time, kings are referred to as 'the Lord's anointed'. Offa had his son Ecgfrith anointed during his own lifetime, the first known anointing of an English king. Charlemagne had recently introduced the ceremony to the Franks.

THE ARCHBISHOP OF LICHFIELD

Offa resented the fact that Kent, now a minor territory, held the metropolitan see of Canterbury. Mercia was the most powerful kingdom. There was a heated argument at a synod in Chelsea. In 788, Lichfield was given the third English archbishopric.

It did not last long. Ten years later another king of Mercia complained to the pope that Gregory's vision of two English provinces had been betrayed. He may have hoped to reactivate Gregory's plan of moving the southern archbishopric to London, which was now in Mercia. If so, his attempt misfired. The pope backed Augustine's tradition. In 803 Lichfield lost its archbishopric. The provincial see remained at Canterbury.

The Celtic controversy persisted. In 816, another synod at Chelsea banned Celtic priests from ministering anywhere in the province of Canterbury.

ALCUIN AT TOURS

As Alcuin grew older, he no longer had the stamina for the high-powered atmosphere of Charlemagne's court. A request to end his days at Echternach or Fulda was turned down. Instead, in 796, he was made abbot of Tours, exchanging the intellectual and political whirlwind for comparative peace.

Charlemagne dragged Alcuin out of this seclusion to dispute against a Spanish heretic. The Spaniard capitulated, but afterwards his colleague, the bishop of Toledo, criticized Alcuin for possessing immense riches, including 20,000 slaves. Alcuin replied, 'It is one to thing to own the world; it is another to be owned by it.' But as he worked on a biography of Martin, founder of western monasticism and the abbey of Tours, Alcuin came to realize the difference between himself and the hermit. Martin had been dragged from his donkey and beaten up, because a gang of soldiers did not recognize an abbot-bishop in rags.

The English in Europe continued to care about their homeland. From his native Northumbria came news of a viking raid on Lindisfarne. Alcuin wrote in grief. How could it happen that Cuthbert's church, the most sacred place in the English lands, is spattered with the blood of its priests and robbed of its treasures? He rebukes the monks for listening to heathen poems and flute-playing in the refectory. What has the hero Ingeld to do with Christ?

There will be a judgement of blood, too, on king and nobles who overdress and overeat, too busy trimming their beards to notice common people dying of cold and starvation. But the brothers of Lindisfarne should take heart. The devastated churches of continental Europe have risen brilliantly from the ashes.

A shadow fell over Alcuin's last years. As his death approached in 804, he begged his friends to pray that, by the mercy of Jesus his Lord, he might 'escape from the dread faces of the Accusing Ones'.

9
Alfred the Great

VIKINGS

Around 789, the reeve of Portland heard news that three foreign ships had landed on this southerly peninsula. Assuming they were merchants, he rode out with a small escort to meet them. He found himself facing the spears of viking raiders. None of his party survived.

'Vikings' were not the whole Scandinavian people. They were raiding bands which set out from the fjords, driven by the pressure of numbers on fertile land and the chance to make a richer living from booty. Those who made for Britain and Ireland were mostly Norwegians or Danes.

Churches and monasteries were treasure troves of precious artefacts. Though monks were not above fighting and dying in defence of them, they were no match for an armed warband. Lindisfarne was particularly vulnerable, a low sandy spit off an otherwise rugged coast. In the summer of 793, the pirates struck. Some brothers fell to axes and swords, others drowned. The survivors fled naked or were taken away into slavery. It was part of a wider onslaught. Along the coast, nuns and monks suffered a similar fate.

The vikings attacked Jarrow the following year. The monks had prepared their defences. They fought off the raiders, aided by a storm which wrecked some Norse ships.

But the wave of pillage and murder could not be stopped, now that the raiders had seen the scale of the booty. Abbots had filled their houses with treasures from across the Christian world. What was meant for the glory of God was an open invitation to heathen looters. Tynemouth and Hartlepool fell victims in 800. In 804, the nuns of Lyminge were given a refuge within the walls of Canterbury.

With coastal monasteries either stripped or preparing their defences, the Norsemen turned their attention to easier pickings in Ireland and France. They returned in force.

The onslaught resumed in earnest when Danes overran the Isle of Sheppey in 835. From Dorset to Lincolnshire it was the same story. For 851, the *Anglo-Saxon Chronicle* records ominously: 'The heathen men stayed over the winter.' The vikings were preparing to settle.

ALFRED'S BOYHOOD

Wessex was now the leading kingdom, in the strongest position to resist the invaders. King Aethelwulf fought off a viking onslaught, but felt prayer was the best hope. In 849, his fifth and favourite child, Alfred, was born. When the boy was only four, his father sent him to Rome where he was given the pope's blessing and the accoutrements of a Roman consul.

His mother Osburgh instilled in him a love of literature. Little Alfred loved to hear Anglo-Saxon poetry recited. One day, Osburgh held up a book of poems. She promised to give it to whichever child should first learn it by heart. 'Will you really?' asked Alfred, in love both with the words and the illuminated letter on the first page. 'Yes, I will,' she smiled. He rushed off with it to his tutor, who read it to him until Alfred was word-perfect. Proudly, he recited the poems to his mother and won the book. She died when he was six.

English texts were by now available. But knowledge of Latin, key to the treasures of scholarship, had dwindled almost to vanishing point. At the court of the leading English king there was no one to teach it. It was a lifelong regret to Alfred that, at the age when he had most time and aptitude for learning, he did not have the right teachers.

His father personally took him back to Rome two years later. They stayed a year. On the return journey, they made another stop. The widowed king married 13-year-old Judith, Charlemagne's great-granddaughter. It was a long absence for a king whose people were suffering constant attacks. But it gave young Alfred a glimpse of a brilliant and intellectual court.

By the time Alfred's father died, sporadic raids had become a campaign of conquest and settlement. In 866, the north was shattered by an attack on York. The precious library of York's school disappears from the records. Churches and monasteries in southern Northumbria were wiped out, Hild's foundation probably among them. The name Whitby, by which we know it now, is Danish. In Mercia, the great inland monastery of Peterborough, a designated pilgrimage site for those who could not make the journey to Rome, burned to the ground.

In 870 Edmund, king of East Anglia, was martyred. The tradition is that Danes surprised him as he lay prostrate in prayer, his weapons laid aside. They bound him to a tree, shot him full of arrows and beheaded him. When his men searched the thickets for the king's lost head, they found a wolf guarding it between its paws. St Edmund was given a greater reverence than other kings who fell in battle against heathens.

KING ALFRED

Then it was Wessex's turn. In 871 Alfred, with his surviving brother King Aethelred, faced the vikings at Ashdown in Berkshire. The Danes charged. King Aethelred refused to leave his tent until his chaplain had finished saying mass. Alfred went out and led the troops.

A few months later, King Aethelred died. He had young children, but the crisis demanded an effective warleader. Alfred was hailed king. He was 22.

He doubted his ability to cope. He was in chronic pain. In his teens, Alfred had been alarmed at his sexual urges. He prayed for some illness to restrain him and developed piles. As an energetic lad who loved hunting, he prayed for an alternative affliction, which would not mar him outwardly nor disable him. The piles were cured, but on his wedding day he was struck with an agonizing pain which doctors were unable to diagnose. He suffered this for the rest of his life. In the rare hours of remission he lived in horror of its return.

Failing to drive them out, Alfred offered the Danes a price to leave Wessex. They occupied London, ravaged Northumbria and marched over Mercia.

The north-east suffered most. The monks of Lindisfarne recognized they were intolerably exposed. In 875, a sad procession crossed the sands to the mainland, bearing with them the remains of Aidan, the coffin containing Cuthbert's body, and the head of King Oswald Bright-Arm. They tried to cross to Ireland, but a storm drove them back. For seven years they wandered from place to place. When the attacks subsided, they established a refuge at Chester-le-Street. Around them, the Danes shared out the conquered farmland and established a viking kingdom. Other vikings made Cambridge their headquarters.

In the midst of this grief, the pope wrote to the archbishops of York and Canterbury urging English clergy to abandon the short tunics of laymen for ankle-length cassocks.

ALFRED'S RETREAT

Alfred's policy of buying off the Danes could not last. Suddenly in 875 he found a Danish army camped at Wareham, in the heart of his kingdom. Again he offered them money to leave. Hostages were exchanged and he made the vikings swear an oath on a ring sacred to Thor. They simply killed the hostages and moved on to Exeter. Alfred drove them out.

Alfred's court spent Christmas at the royal residence of Chippenham. Just after their Twelfth Night celebrations, the vikings caught them unawares. Now Alfred was on the run, with a small company. He found a hiding place in the salt marshes of the Somerset Levels, on Athelney, 'Island of the Princes'. They lived like brigands, snatching food from the vikings, or even their own people.

Legend says he sheltered in a swineherd's cottage. The housewife set some loaves to bake and busied herself at the other end of the room. Alfred was so sunk in contemplating his misfortunes that he failed to notice the bread was burning. When the woman looked up and saw the smoke, she gave him a piece of her mind. 'You won't turn the loaves when they're burning in front of your nose, but you're glad enough to eat them when they come out of the oven!' Shaken, Alfred buckled down to help her after that. True or not, it is an acute commentary on the need Alfred realized to help the common people.

RESTORING THE KINGDOM

Alfred emerged from his guerrilla camp to win a decisive battle at Edington on the Wiltshire Downs. The Danish leader, Guthrum, consented to be baptized at Aller, the nearest church to Athelney, with Alfred as his godfather. A treaty was drawn up respecting English and Danish rights, with an agreed boundary between them. The Danes kept possession of Northumbria, the east midlands, East Anglia and Essex, a region known later as the Danelaw. Alfred ruled all southern Britain, with western Mercia recognizing his overlordship.

Alfred's care for his people took the enduring form of a network of burghs, fortified towns, across southern England. Ancient fortresses were strengthened, new towns founded. They were sited to guard strategic routes, with the intention that most people would live within 20 miles of a refuge. The surrounding parishes contributed taxation, labour and guard duties. It forced neighbouring communities to cooperate.

RESTORING THE CHURCH

The Church had suffered greatly in these wars. Abbeys, cathedral churches and minsters, once powerhouses for pastoral care, missionary endeavour and learning. were prime targets. In the countryside, simple parish churches, little monasteries and remote hermitages may have suffered less. But the Church's infrastructure was gone. Libraries were lost, schools scattered, teachers killed. Many people turned back to heathen beliefs, hidden from view when baptism became compulsory.

With his borders secure, Alfred turned his attention to building up the Church. Alfred's passion was not for religious professionals, but for widespread Christian learning. He wanted his court to be like Charlemagne's. He was a dedicated student himself, making up for the deficiencies of his boyhood by spending all the spare time he could snatch in study. Wessex, which had once boasted Aldhelm and Boniface, was short of teachers. He brought four English scholars from Mercia.

Next, Alfred sent a letter to the archbishop of Rheims requesting an ageing scholar, Grimbald, then a monk in Flanders, and accompanying his plea with a present of wolfhounds. He gets what he wants, grudgingly. The archbishop regards the English as barbarians. He demands oaths that they will give Grimbald the respect he deserves. His patronizing letter derides a degenerate English Church with irregular practices.

Grimbald himself was a humble man, a fine musician, respected for his biblical scholarship and upright life. He turned down the offer of the archbishopric of Canterbury, recommending Alfred's Mercian scholar Plegmund instead. He stayed a simple teacher and priest at Winchester, living communally in the clergy-house.

Monasteries were declining in influence and spirituality, even before the viking raids. Alfred founded only two, though he made gifts to others. The time of double monasteries had passed. He installed his 15-year-old daughter Aethelgifu as abbess of a nunnery at his newly created town of Shaftesbury. He genuinely believed in the leadership abilities of his teenage daughters. On the island of Athelney, where he had found refuge, Alfred founded a monastery for men.

John from Old Saxony was given the unpopular job of abbot. Athelney's significance to Alfred was lost on other people. The island was surrounded by swamps and reached only by punt or wooden causeway. Enthusiasm for remote, damp sites had long since dwindled. No English monks wanted to live there. It was only filled by recruiting from continental Europe and by child-oblates, who had no say in the matter.

Two monks from Gaul became so embittered that they plotted murder. It is said they planned to dump the abbot's body on the doorstep of a local whore. The abbot used to pray alone in the church at night. They laid in wait for him. But John was an alert man, trained in martial arts. He heard them move before their weapons struck. His shout of alarm brought the brothers rushing into the church, where their unarmed abbot was putting up a brave fight. John survived, severely wounded.

In 885 Alfred invited a Welshman to his Winchester court. Asser was a priest at St David's, possibly its abbot. His monastery was reluctant to lose him. It was arranged that Asser should spend six months of the year with Alfred and six at St David's. After eight months in Wessex, he was still pressing Alfred for permission to leave. Alfred responded by giving him two monasteries, a silk cloak and a quantity of incense 'weighing as much as a stout man'.

Asser soon had Alfred improving his Latin and working his way through the Bible. One day, Asser read out a passage to him to illustrate a point. The king took out a little book he always carried and asked Asser to copy this passage into it. Asser saw the book contained the daily services, some psalms and other prayers Alfred knew. But there was no room left. The king was urging him to hurry up. Asser suggested starting a new sheet. 'Who knows? We may find more passages you like, and then you'll be glad to have them all together.' He quickly made an eight-page booklet. It went everywhere with Alfred and rapidly filled.

ALFRED'S BOOKS

Alfred was hardly typical of the laity. But he cared about them. Books were not just for the clergy. The laity should be active participants in a Christian kingdom. He wanted to restore lost knowledge and increase the number who could read it in Latin. But to reach more of his subjects, he realized, works needed to be available in English too. As he started to read Latin himself, he conceived the idea of a programme of translation, beginning with the early Christian classics. What is more, he took on a share of the translation himself, though he readily confesses that he was helped by better scholars.

Alfred's own first assignment was Gregory's *Pastoral Care*, a standard work for bishops and priests. It advocates personal prayer in solitude, coupled with unceasing work for the souls entrusted to the pastor's care. This 'Shepherd-book' is an expression of Alfred's own spirituality and sense of responsibility for his people.

Alfred's preface says that at the start of his reign he knew of no one south of the Thames with enough Latin to understand church services or translate a letter. He believed there were very few elsewhere. The charge is exaggerated, but it shows the startling decline from the eighth century, when monks, nuns and clergy wrote books in Latin and corresponded enthusiastically with scholarly colleagues. Without learning and teaching, Alfred says, 'We were Christians in name alone'. Every bishop in Alfred's territory will receive a copy, which must be always in use. It comes with a jewelled bookmark. The Alfred Jewel, found near Athelney, may be one such. A rock crystal, set in gold, encloses a figure who is perhaps Christ in Wisdom. The edge is inscribed: 'Alfred had me made'. Alfred aims wider still. In peacetime, every freeborn boy with sufficient intelligence should learn to read. For most, this must be in English, but young men suitable for holy orders will graduate to Latin.

His translations grow freer. Lady Philosophy becomes biblical Wisdom, our comforter in extreme suffering. He begins adding his own insights, even diverging completely from the text of Augustine of Hippo's *Soliloquies*. There was so much he needed to say and do.

He brings away from this 'forest' of many authors, 'the finest timbers I could carry' to build a splendid house. Like his subjects, a king needs tools and materials to carry out his craft. A king's tools are the threefold division of society: those who pray, fight and work.

At the time of his death he was working on an English version of the Psalter. Many psalms are attributed to King David. Alfred evidently took him as a role model.

Court translators made Bede's religious history of the English people available to them in their own language. Another great contribution of Alfred's reign was the *Anglo-Saxon Chronicle*, though it may not have been written at his court. This compilation records the history of the Anglo-Saxon people year by year. Others continued it and produced regional versions.

Asser wrote his *Life of Alfred* apparently for a Welsh readership. He commends Alfred, their overlord, as the defender of Christianity, referring to the English army as 'the Christians'.

The writing of a *Life* is significant. There was already a *Life of Charlemagne* which is likely to have influenced Asser. But in Britain, until now, this genre had been reserved for saints.

ALFRED AND THE LAITY

Besides schools for the young, Alfred saw the need to catch up on Wessex's wasted years through adult education. He could only govern this huge territory effectively if those exercising power under him had access to written instructions. Shire ealdormen, district reeves and local thanes must all learn to read, if they wanted to keep their jobs. If the task proved genuinely too much, they must appoint someone to read aloud to them. The administrators complied, 'sighing deeply from the bottom of their hearts'. Alfred believed in the laity.

Alfred attended mass daily. He also observed the canonical hours day and night, like a monk. He carried his handbook of prayers and spiritual thoughts, adding new devotional material he discovered. He decided to dedicate half his time and half his income to God. Shares went to the poor, the palace school, his two monastic foundations, Athelney and Shaftesbury, and churches, not only in Wessex, but from Ireland to Gaul.

It was a breathtaking achievement, the 'lone helmsman' steering the ship of his kingdom, 'though all his sailors were virtually exhausted'. He hired craftsmen from abroad. He personally oversaw the work of builders, goldsmiths, falconers, kennelmen. His vow to devote half his hours to God was frustrated by the difficulty of measuring time at night or on cloudy days. He invented the candle-clock, with the hours marked on a 12-inch length of wax. Unfortunately, as he travelled round his kingdom, his churches and tents proved too draughty for the candles to burn evenly. Alfred devised the horn lantern. At every turn, his Christianity took practical form.

In cases involving the poor, Alfred was an astute and painstaking judge. They saw him as their only champion. He accused the wealthy nobles of caring only for their own self-interest.

Alfred turned his attention to a code of laws. He saw them as continuing a tradition that stretched back to Moses. His fundamental tenet was loyalty to one's lord. God, he says, has commanded everyone to love his earthly lord as he loves heaven's Lord. But Anglo-Saxons were allowed to choose which lord they would serve, though a change might involve considerable cost to the new lord.

Under Alfred, peace was established between Danes and English. The Danish settlers liked what they saw and rapidly became Christians.

Alfred the Great died in 899. His greatness was in offering great things to ordinary people.

THE LADY OF THE MERCIANS

His work was continued in Wessex by his son Edward the Elder and in Mercia by his remarkable eldest daughter Aethelfled, 'Lady of the Mercians'. She shared her father's vision of an England made peaceful by treaties and commerce, rather than wars, yet secured by defended towns to which all had access.

She was about 15 when she married Aethelred, the ealdorman ruling Mercia. Lady Aethelfled joined in top-level councils and the couple were jointly acknowledged 'lords' of Mercia. They extended Alfred's policy, fortifying burghs for the Mercians. They built Oxford. They renewed the Roman cities of Worcester and Gloucester, where paths had run over heaps of rubble. They laid out street plans to make movement easier. Burghs had a fourfold purpose: defence, administration, commerce and Christianity. They unified scattered people and bound neighbouring kingdoms in a common interest, including, in time, the Danes.

Lady Aethelfled caused new churches to be built in her burghs. While others dedicated churches to Peter or Mary, she had an enthusiasm for English saints. Gloucester's minster she named for a distant ancestor, St Oswald of Northumbria, who founded Lindisfarne. She brought his relics here from Bardney. Like her father, Oswald Bright-Arm was a layman, who fought a decisive battle to save his country from heathens.

At their new town of Shrewsbury, Lady Aethelfled dedicated her church to St Alkmund, another Northumbrian. She was insisting to her people that English men and women could rise to sainthood.

When vikings expelled from Dublin landed in the north-west, Ealdorman Aethelred was ill. The Lady of the Mercians met the viking leader. He said his people were 'weary of war' and wanted to settle down. Aethelfled took a calculated risk and gave them land. But when the vikings recovered, they attacked Chester. Lady Aethelfled led her army against them and won. The vikings accepted her rule. She fortified Chester and made it a thriving commercial centre, open to English, Danes, Norwegians, Welsh, Irish and Franks. Her church here was dedicated to St Werburg, a Mercian princess and abbess.

In 909, her brother King Edward the Elder attacked the northern Danelaw, shattering the earlier peace Alfred had negotiated. The result was a vicious counter-attack on Mercia, which Edward put down with wholesale slaughter. That left the north-west defenceless. Norse invaders from Ireland moved in and set up a stronger Scandinavian kingdom based on York.

When Ealdorman Aethelred died in 911, leaving only a daughter, the Mercians hailed Lady Aethelfled as sole ruler and commander of the army, 'with rightful lordship holding Mercian rule'. She continued her father's work with undiminished energy, building or reconstructing nine more towns. Where Normans later built castles to defend themselves against the people, she built walls to defend the people. Three times she commanded the army successfully in the field. She won, not by playing the heroic warrior, but by intelligent strategy. She led her army against a Welsh king who had killed a Mercian abbot and his monks, and in defence of Wales when a viking force landed. She led an alliance with the Scots and the British of Strathclyde to assist the suffering Northumbrians.

In 917, she attacked Derby. Its vikings submitted to her rule and she gained the relics of St Alkmund for Shrewsbury. Then the vikings of Leicester acknowledged her without a fight. The model of cooperation she was demonstrating at Chester showed her rule could be prosperous for both sides. In 918, she had her greatest coup in sight. The new Norse rulers in York pledged allegiance to her. But she died that summer and was buried at St Oswald's in Gloucester beside Aethelred. The

Mercians chose her daughter to succeed her. But the king of Wessex, Edward the Elder, seized power from his niece and confined her to a nunnery. The trust between English and vikings collapsed.

The tenth-century poem 'Judith' tells of the heroine of the Apocrypha, who risks her life to deliver her people. It probably celebrates the Lady of the Mercians.

Alfred the Great and Lady Aethelfled envisioned an English Church both caring for and enabling the laity. By shared defence, education, the inspiration of the English saints and offering the hand of peace to the invaders, they showed how it might be possible to build a Christian kingdom.

10

Monastic Revival and Sacred Kingship

DUNSTAN'S YOUTH

The tenth century saw the revival of the monastic ideal and a vision of sacred kingship. The key lay in the career of Dunstan.

Dunstan was born around 909, some five miles from Glastonbury. His family were well connected to court and church. His uncle Athelm was the first bishop of Wells. Glastonbury was then an island in a marshy bay opening on to the Bristol Channel. It had been a Celtic monastery before King Ine refounded it with English monks. The Irish saints Brigid and Aidan were thought to be buried there, as well as the British Gildas and the Northumbrian Ceolfrith. Irish pilgrims came, bringing their scholarship.

Here Dunstan came to be schooled. He showed a talent for calligraphy, as well as designing and executing paintings and metalwork. He became an accomplished poet and musician. When Uncle Athelm became archbishop of Canterbury, he invited the teenage Dunstan to join his church 'family'.

In 925 his uncle crowned Athelstan, Alfred's grandson, king of Wessex. Victory over the Norse kingdom of York made him the first king of all England. He completed the conquest of Cornwall. The independent Cornish Church finally submitted to the authority of Canterbury.

Athelstan's laws decreed that any commoner who owned four hides of bookland and a defended site with church, kitchen, bell-house and gate-house, could be promoted to the rank of thane. The number of parish churches increased. Baptisms had been mass celebrations held annually at central locations. Now baptism could be delegated to parishes. Fonts began to appear, first wooden tubs perhaps, then stone.

Uncle Athelm recommended Dunstan to Athelstan's court. Here he heard a very old man telling of the martyrdom of his king, Edmund of East Anglia, shot full of viking arrows. The account brought tears running down the boy's face. King Athelstan had Edmund's remains transferred to Bury St Edmunds.

Charlemagne's successors were now Holy Roman Emperors. Many of Athelstan's relatives married into this family. Kingship was gaining in sanctity.

Dunstan's love of heroic Anglo-Saxon lays got him into trouble. Fellow courtiers reported him to the king for heathenism. But they sentenced him themselves at a kangaroo court and threw him, roped, into a hog-pit. Dunstan managed to haul himself out and staggered to a friend's house. He was so covered with stinking mud that the dogs rushed at him, barking ferociously. He succeeded in calming them and remarked that they were friendlier than his human companions.

Another kinsman, Aelfheah the Bald, was the new monk-bishop of Winchester. Aelfheah tried to persuade Dunstan to take a monk's vows. Dunstan protested with horror that he would rather marry his girlfriend than dress in 'sheep's rags'. Aelfheah persisted. An acute attack of piles decided Dunstan. He became a monk in Aelfheah the Bald's community.

Here he met his lifelong friend Aethelwold. Both were accomplished metalworkers. They were ordained priests on the same day.

CONTRASTING MONASTERIES

Aelfheah the Bald's community was ascetic. Others were not. When Oda the Good became archbishop of Canterbury, he helped his nephew Oswald buy an independent monastery in Winchester. Here Oswald dressed in silk and lived like a courtier, popular with the married minster clergy.

Monasteries at that time were often little more than tax avoidance schemes. The frequent reminders of the prohibition of sexual intercourse with nuns is not the stuff of Sunday tabloids. Nuns could be single or married women, wearing secular dress, living lives indistinguishable from other women's.

119

Their celibacy could not be taken for granted. Fulminations against depraved and licentious clergy may simply mean they were married men living with their wives and families. On the continent there was now a revival of the monastic ideal. It sprang from the Benedictine houses of Cluny and Fleury. Young Oswald grew disillusioned with his monastery and left for Fleury.

Dunstan was now spending longer periods back at Glastonbury, studying and teaching. There was a widow hermit living in a hut near the ancient church. Dunstan respected her deeply and she became his spiritual director. She gave him financial support as well.

He still painted. He designed embroidery and played the harp to local women as they stitched it. There is a tradition that Dunstan was metal-working when the devil tormented him with memories of past girlfriends. Dunstan's response was to tweak his nose with red-hot tongs. The devil fled shrieking, 'Look what the bald fellow's done to me!'

BENEDICTINE REFORM

When Athelstan died, his half-brother King Edmund invited Dunstan back to court. The court was at Cheddar when accusations were again laid against him. King Edmund lost his temper and ordered Dunstan to be stripped of all honours and go as far away as possible. Frankish envoys suggested he would be better off with them. While Dunstan was finalizing his plans for emigration, the king went hunting over the Mendip Hills. In front of him the stag suddenly disappeared. Next moment, so did the hounds. King Edmund was in full gallop after them when his horse pulled up violently. Beneath them, a cliff plunged down into Cheddar Gorge. The shaken king took this as a divine warning. He rode back and summoned Dunstan. Together they went to Glastonbury's ancient church, prayed and embraced. Edmund led Dunstan by the hand and set him in the abbot's chair.

King Edmund's most interesting contribution to the Church was his appointment in 941 of Oda the Good as archbishop of

Canterbury. Oda's father was a Dane. Some ten years later, his Danish relative Oskytel became archbishop of York. Children of viking converts were now leading the English Church.

Dunstan established the Rule of Benedict at Glastonbury. He appointed his brother to administer the abbey's estates, since those who had taken monastic vows were 'unsuited to pursue secular matters'. The monks devoted their energies to teaching, supplying high-ranking clergy.

To his joy, his friend Aethelwold came to join him. Aethelwold wanted to continue his training overseas, but the Queen Mother said he was too good a man to be allowed to leave the country. Instead, he was offered the deserted abbey of Abingdon. It had been an Irish monastery, then an English one. Now it was refounded, with more estates. The new king Eadred was so keen on the plan, he came to measure out the foundations. Afterwards the king's party dined in the refectory, and went on downing mead until many were stone drunk.

Aethelwold sent a monk to Fleury to learn about the Benedictine reformation. He returned advocating an emphasis on liturgy and independence from local secular control.

King Edwy the Fair was 15 when he was crowned at Kingston-on-Thames. In the middle of his coronation banquet he rushed off to his mistress's bed. Archbishop Oda the Good appealed for someone to fetch him back. Nobody wanted to risk the new king's displeasure. It fell to Dunstan and the bishop of Lichfield.

They found the jewelled crown tossed on the floor. The king was in bed, not only with his mistress but her daughter as well. The bishops summoned him to return. The king refused. Dunstan dragged him out of bed, put the crown back on his head and returned him forcibly to the hall.

It was not, in the short term, a good career move. Edwy married the younger mistress. At Glastonbury, discontent had fomented in Dunstan's absence. The king stripped him of the abbey and his personal property, breaking the terms of King Edmund's grant to him. Dunstan fled to a monastery in Ghent. Here he found further evidence of Benedictine reform.

A Reforming Archbishop

When Oda the Good died, the next archbishop of Canterbury set out for Rome to receive the *pallium*. In the tenth century, English archbishops took a pride in receiving their investiture personally from the pope. A century later, they complained about the difficulty and expense of the journey. This English archbishop was caught in a blizzard in the Alps. In vain, his companions tried to warm him by slitting open the belly of his horse and putting his feet inside. He froze to death.

The next king, Edgar the Peaceable, recalled Dunstan from exile. When the primacy was again vacant, Dunstan was enthroned as archbishop of Canterbury. He too set out on the arduous journey to Rome. Dunstan's steward lost patience when supplies ran low on the way. He blamed the archbishop for giving so much away in alms. Dunstan tried to soothe him, until the bell rang for vespers. The steward shouted after him, 'That's right! Go off and adore that Christ of yours, who doesn't bother about what we need.' Dunstan had hardly started to sing the office before messengers arrived. A friendly abbot had been awaiting their arrival and sent all the delicacies his region could provide.

Archbishop Dunstan was influential at court. Edgar the Peaceable's law code made binding the tradition of 'plough-alms' at Easter, 'church-scot' at harvest-time, and 'soul-scot' for burials. This income strengthened the parish churches. Parish clergy were to teach children manual skills. Parishioners were also required to pay the 'hearth penny' on St Peter's day, sent to support the papal see. Late payers were supposed to take the money to Rome themselves, with a substantial surcharge, obtain a receipt, and on return to pay a colossal fine to the king. This must have been difficult to enforce.

It was a time of building. As a child, Dunstan had climbed on to the roof of Glastonbury's church in the delirium of fever. He was found inside, sleeping between two workmen, with the church door still shut. As an adult, he was nearly crushed when a stone fell from the roof of the church where he was sitting. Dunstan donated organs to churches. He gave bells. English churches were now being built with strong square towers to support them.

Dunstan wanted to be a reforming archbishop. His programme spread north with the return of Oswald from Fleury. In 958, Oswald heard that his uncle Archbishop Oda the Good was dying, but he landed in Dover too late. He was about to return when he was persuaded to contact another Danish kinsman, Archbishop Oskytel of York. Oskytel offered Oswald the bishopric of Worcester.

Dunstan himself appointed his friend Aethelwold, abbot of Abingdon, to the powerful see of Winchester. These three were monks, unusual for a bishop then. They planned to run cathedrals like monasteries, centres of learning, staffed by men of purity, lifting the morals and morale of both laity and secular clergy.

AETHELWOLD AT WINCHESTER

The Anglo-Celtic Church had been based on monasteries. Augustine and Theodore had worked from a non-monastic community at Canterbury cathedral. Alfred and his family built minsters in their new burghs. A minster was a central mission church with a community of clergy, a spiritual burgh. At Winchester there was Alfred's Old Minster, the New Minster built by his son, and the Nunnaminster, founded for women by Alfred's widow. These minsters had succumbed to the same failings as the monasteries. Unfortunately, we learn about them only through the criticism of celibate monks, who deplored the idea of clergy living like the laity.

Aethelwold arrived at Winchester after a serious injury. He had been working on a building at Abingdon when a huge post collapsed. It knocked him into a pit, smashing most of his ribs on one side.

At Winchester he censured the secular clergy of the Old Minster for gluttony, drunkenness and lechery. This may indicate simply his abhorrence of married clergy. For months they put off change. One Saturday evening, the clergy were singing an antiphon which includes the words, 'Take hold on discipline'. As the service finished, the bishop appeared in the cathedral, backed by monks from Abingdon, who threw monastic cowls on the floor in front of the minster clergy. Aethelwold gave them a straight choice: adopt the discipline of monastic life or find another job. 'Tomorrow,' they pleaded. 'Now!' he insisted. The clergy left in fury. Besides a different outlook, many of them had wives and families. After consideration, three returned as monks. Aethelwold replaced the rest with celibates from Abingdon.

It was risky. Many he had sacked had powerful connections. Aethelwold's drink was poisoned. Pain gripped his bowels and he staggered from the table to his bed. Then he reproached himself. Had not Christ told his disciples they could take deadly drink without it harming them? He got up, put on a cheerful face and returned to the hall.

With the king's backing, he next reformed the New Minster. Clergy are to have no dealings with the business or society of the city. They must eat together and not admit strangers to their refectory. They are to welcome the poor with open arms but otherwise lead lives of prayer and study. For the Nunnaminster, he appointed as abbess an elderly family friend with a reputation for holiness. She instilled a stricter discipline. Aethelwold decided all three communities should be grouped in a single enclosure, to minimize land disputes between them and cut out disturbance from noisy neighbours. To achieve this, he pulled down the offending citizens' houses, with the king's backing.

In the Old Minster cemetery lay the body of St Swithun. Tradition says he was a humble ninth-century bishop, who asked not to be buried in the cathedral, but to lie out of doors under the grass, where the rain would fall on him and the feet of common people walk over his grave. Aethelwold constructed a vast extension housing a grander tomb. It was linked to the Old Minster and surrounded with chapels. The new building was so complex, some people could not find their way out. The day the saint's coffin was to be moved, it rained so hard that the ceremony had to be put off. It went on raining for 40 days, proof, some said, of the saint's indignation at the move. A counter story then circulated that Swithun had appeared to a smith with the message that he wished his bones to be translated into the church, the mark of sainthood. It began a healing cult. The church was left so many crutches and stools from those who had been cured that there was no room to hang them all up. The overworked choir monks regretted their commitment to singing the *Te Deum* whenever anyone was healed.

Aethelwold himself struggled against pain. He suffered from diarrhoea and leg problems, and spent sleepless nights. During the day, his indomitable spirit kept him active, but affliction showed in his pale, gaunt face. He ate no meat or poultry. Once he was so ill that Dunstan ordered him to take a more nourishing diet for three months. In old age, his eyesight was failing. But he still read far into the night, blinking his eyes repeatedly to clear his vision. Once a brother looked in on him and found him asleep, the candle overturned and the page alight.

Aethelwold also filled the lapsed abbey of Ely with monks. They honoured its founder, the resolutely virgin queen Aethelthryth, popularly called Audrey. The remains of her sisters, Seaxburg and Witburg, were reburied beside her. But there were no nuns at Ely now. He rebuilt Peterborough and founded Thorney nearby.

OSWALD OF YORK

Oswald of Worcester shared Dunstan and Aethelwold's vision of reforming cathedral chapters along Benedictine lines. But he was not the autocrat that Aethelwold was. When he arrived as bishop, his sermons drew such crowds that he had to preach from the base of a grave cross in the cemetery. He sent to Fleury, where he had studied, for a monk to teach the Rule. When he met determined opposition, he moved his reformers to a temporary monastery near Bristol. He changed the cathedral personnel gradually, as vacancies occurred. An idealistic ealdorman caught his vision. To help Oswald realize his ideals more quickly, he gave him land and money to found a new house at Ramsey, in the East Anglian fens. Here he could have a reformed Benedictine abbey, training a new generation. The laity were divided over the reforms.

In 972, Oswald was made archbishop of York, but he kept the bishopric of Worcester. The York see was so impoverished by viking depredations that it had become customary to hold the two jointly. Worcester was rich. Oswald had a huge land-holding, known as the Oswaldlow, which he leased out to a wide range of people. In return, the lessees pledged themselves to accept only his authority and the king's. Oswald was the lord to some 10,000 people.

Three-quarters of the bishops Dunstan consecrated were monks, most from Glastonbury, others Aethelwold's protégés from Winchester or Abingdon. A few were Oswald's men. The wholesale changes were having a visible effect. The laity experienced a new urge to piety.

THE AGREEMENT ON THE RULE

Queen Aethelthryth commissioned Aethelwold of Winchester to translate the Rule of Benedict for one of her nunneries. It led to a great council at Winchester in the early 970s. This was attended by monastic bishops, abbots and abbesses, and representatives from the continental Benedictine houses which had influenced Aethelwold and Oswald.

Under Dunstan's guidance, they drew up the 'Agreement on the Rule'. It was a compendium of reformed Benedictine practices, which would take precedence over local custom and which they would all accept.

Church and monarch will support each other. The king will protect the men's monasteries, the queen the nunneries. Abbots, but not abbesses, will sit in the witan. The monasteries will offer masses and prayers for the royal family, which must not be chanted at excessive speed. Communities will elect their own abbot, but with the 'consent and advice' of the king. They will have the king's ear, but are forbidden to associate with other people of importance for meals, inside or outside the monastery. Lay nobles have no power over them. They are not to hoard wealth for taxes, but use it to care for the poor.

The vowed religious must observe the canonical hours. If on a journey, they must dismount and get down on their knees. They should, in any case, not gad about. Worship is their prime purpose. Children entrusted to them are not to be hugged or kissed. No monk must ever be alone with a young boy. They are to be hospitable to the needy and strangers and, unique to England, wash the feet of some poor people every day in Lent.

The reformers' emphasis on liturgy went far beyond Benedict's original Rule. Monks now spent most of their time in corporate worship, rather than balancing this with personal devotions, study and manual work. They might be in church for five hours before daybreak. Manual work was usually done by servants.

There were more extensive services for Holy Week, including our earliest Easter play. A monk wearing an alb, a white smock, enters. He goes to the shrouded tomb of Christ and sits, holding a palm branch. Separately, three others wearing copes enter. They carry incense burners. As they search, the one in white asks, 'Who are you looking for, women of Christ?' They reply, 'Jesus of Nazareth'. The angel tells them, 'He is not here, but has risen as he promised. Go and proclaim his resurrection from the dead.' The three turn, chanting, 'Alleluia! The Lord has risen.' The angel invites them, 'Come and see the place.' He lifts the veil, showing the tomb empty save for the linen wrappings. The three take these up to the altar and sing their affirmation, 'The Lord is risen from the tomb.'

Particularly English concerns were the veneration of the cross and the ringing of bells at Christmas. Monks were to process to their local parish church to honour its patron saint.

During his reign, King Edgar ordered the foundation of 50 new monasteries, compared with Alfred's two. In return, the monks vowed loyalty to the king and his bishops, and prayers for king and country. The king told the bishops, 'You hold Peter's sword and I hold Constantine's. Let us join sword to sword, drive the lepers out of our camp, and cleanse the Lord's sanctuary. We want only Levites as ministers in the Church, who are ready to tell their parents, "I do not know you".'

EDGAR'S CORONATION

Edgar the Peaceable had become king at 16. But he was approaching 30 before he underwent his coronation ceremony, the age when a man could be ordained priest. It was a consecration of such solemnity that King Edgar effectively ceased to function as a layman. The service was conducted by both archbishops at Bath in 973.

Edgar was first shown to the people, wearing his crown, for their acclamation. Then he bared his head and prostrated himself before the altar. He rose to make the 'King's Promise', drawn up by Dunstan and used at all future coronations. The monarch swore, in the name of the Holy Trinity, 'to the Christian people and my subjects', that he would uphold the peace of the Church and all Christian folk, forbid robbery and other crimes to all ranks, and rule with justice and mercy, that the God of mercy 'may forgive us all'. Dunstan's prayer of consecration proclaimed him king of 'all Albion', or Britain. He was anointed with oil, spiritual power, to the words: 'Zadok the priest and Nathan the prophet anointed Solomon king.' The people shouted in reply, 'May the king live for ever!' Dunstan placed the ring of sound faith on Edgar's finger and girded him with a sword to defend the Church in the power of the Holy Spirit. Then he set the crown of God's blessing on his head. Edgar was handed the sceptre of kingly power, with a prayer that God would honour him above all the kings in Britain, and the rod of virtue and justice. After mass, both king and queen, probably also anointed, were led to their thrones. The queen then feasted separately from the king, entertaining the abbots and abbesses.

This is a sacred kingship. An illustration in Aethelwold's *Benedictional*, drawn by his chaplain, sheds light on the thinking behind this impressive ceremony. It shows Christ, King of kings, shedding light on England's king. The linking of Lord and lord, which underpins Anglo-Saxon spirituality, is here made visible.

The image of Christ the King is central to Christian iconography at this time. In the Winchester school of illumination, the emphasis shifts from rich decoration to line drawing, from fabulous beasts to human figures, caught in lifelike poses of action and emotion. King Edgar dances with the angels as he offers his charter to the New Minster. The *Benedictional* is the first to show a crowned Christ being offered gifts by crowned magi. The 'wise men' of the New Testament have become monarchs. One of them offers his crown to the Christ Child. Another groundbreaking picture is the coronation of the Virgin Mary.

Bishops themselves were enthroned like kings in their cathedrals.

11

Who Shall Be King?

EDWARD THE MARTYR

Two years after this magnificent ceremony, Edgar the Peaceable died and was buried at Glastonbury. Glorious certainty evaporated in confusion over the succession. Edward the Martyr was the son of Edgar's first wife, or, some said, of a nun whom King Edgar had taken from Wilton Abbey for his concubine. Edward was 16 and feared for his violent rages. The choice was between him and ten-year-old Aethelred, son of Edgar and his queen Aethelthryth. Archbishops Dunstan and Oswald crowned Edward at Kingston-upon-Thames.

There was unrest in the midlands and the north. Old resentments against the reformers surfaced. Monasteries were plundered. Some monks were ejected from minsters and married clergy took back their posts. Matters came to a head when the witan assembled at Calne. Dunstan was now an old man, so ill that he had to conduct business from a stretcher, standing only to pray. Unable to reach an agreed verdict, he resorted to prayer. The floor of the hall collapsed, leaving Dunstan balanced on a beam. Others were severely or fatally injured.

Ealdorman Aethelwine of East Anglia had built Oswald an abbey at Ramsey. When the new tower cracked from top to bottom, he cheerfully paid for another. He now came to the monastic party's defence at an East Anglian council. His brother even killed a man trying to seize land from Peterborough Abbey. The reformers secured their estates, but their credibility had been dented.

The young king called on King Edgar's widow, Queen Aethelthryth, at Corfe. Those who came out to greet him dragged Edward from his horse and stabbed him. His body was ignominiously buried. Suspicion fell on his half-brother Aethelred's supporters.

There was talk of making the murdered king's sister Edith monarch. Edith was certainly the daughter of Edgar the Peaceable and his concubine. Her mother had returned to Wilton, where she spent the rest of her life as a nun, taking the baby with her. Edith grew up there, well educated by tutors from the continent. Though she lived as a nun, Bishop Aethelwold of Winchester rebuked her for the richness of her clothes. Edith retorted that pride can be found clad in rags, and her own mind 'may be as pure under these vestments as under your tattered furs'. The monk-bishop was reduced to blushes.

Her father had offered Edith prestigious abbacies, but she declined, suggesting other candidates. Nothing came of the idea of monarchy either. Instead, Edith commissioned an oratory with a series of paintings depicting her brother's murder. The unpleasant young man who had terrorized his servants became revered as Edward the Martyr.

AETHELRED EVIL-COUNSEL

Despite the rumours, the boy Aethelred was acclaimed king and consecrated by Dunstan within a month. Dunstan is said to have given him a severe lecture about the shady start to his reign.

Aethelwold of Winchester attempted to act as Aethelred's mentor, but he died in 984. The 18-year-old king surrounded himself with wild young noblemen, including the bishop of Ramsey. They looted church lands. The bishop of Rochester put up a spirited fight. The king laid siege to Rochester. Failing to break in, he devastated the diocese around. Dunstan tried to intervene, but had to buy him off.

His nickname 'Aethelred the Unready' is an Anglo-Saxon pun. 'Raed' means 'Counsel'. 'Aethelred Unraed' translates as 'Noble-Counsel Evil-Counsel'. The feelings of his people for him are summed up in the story that, when Dunstan lowered the baby prince into the font for baptism, little Aethelred emptied his bowels into the holy water. Dunstan lost his temper and predicted he would turn out a 'sorry fellow'.

The archbishop was in his late seventies and spending more time in his community at Canterbury. Dunstan the musician had enhanced the liturgy of the English Church. Now he dreamed of angel choirs. He experienced visions as he recited the night-office. Next morning, Dunstan awoke with a clear memory of heavenly music. He dictated the hymns, then taught the cathedral clergy and monks to sing them.

In 988, on the feast of the Ascension, he preached his last sermon 'as he had never preached before'. It was the message of salvation, from the Son who had risen to live with the Father and the Spirit for eternity. He shared the midday meal with the brothers, then retired for a siesta. When he did not reappear, monks went to rouse him. They found him in bed, 'his bald head gleaming'. He did not have the strength to rise and died two days later, singing Psalm 111, 'He has gained renown by his wonderful deeds; the Lord provides food for those who fear him.' It sums up Anglo-Saxon Christianity: the mutual pact between Lord and follower.

Four years later, Oswald of York died. His end epitomized his revival of purity and charity. It was the reformers' custom to wash the feet of 12 poor men every day throughout Lent. Oswald stooped to wipe them with his own hair. He sang 15 psalms, holding the basin. Then, as he genuflected for the benediction, he collapsed and died. He had come a long way from that convivial young man in silk at his dubious monastery in Winchester.

Under Dunstan, Aethelwold and Oswald, the Church had been rescued from degeneracy and decay. In the process, monasteries and minsters had grown immensely rich. Parish clergy, like most of their parishioners, remained poor. There is no suggestion that these men sought personal profit. Ascetic spirituality was at the heart of their reforms.

These three were statesmen as well as bishops. National decision-making was part of the Church's mission. They gave English monarchy back its pre-Christian sacredness. King and Church legitimized each other.

Aelfric and the Millennium

Aelfric was a scholar. He was educated at Winchester and wrote the lives of bishops Aethelwold and Swithun of that city. Alfred the Great's faith in a literate laity had borne fruit. Aelfric often wrote translations and treatises at the request of laymen.

Aelfric also wrote sermons for parish priests. He warns against heathenism. Women should keep away from cross-roads, where some dedicate themselves and their children to the devil. He fears the Anglo-Saxon fatalism, tempting them to accept evil as their inevitable 'wyrd'. Aelfric has his own sense of Doomsday. He sees guilty souls, bound and hanging on an immense cliff over black water. Fog swirls, monsters lurk, devils snatch at them like wolves. Then the twigs they cling to snap, plunging them down to the waiting mouths.

In sculpture, the figure of Christ in majesty is beginning to give way to the suffering Jesus on the cross. With more viking threats and the millennium approaching, the Anglo-Saxons had a dark view of what lay ahead. But Aelfric does not approve of priests and monks taking up weapons. He writes of the urgent need for 'good teaching, in this age which is the end of the world'.

He inserts a heartfelt plea at the end of his preface to a book of sermons. Will anyone who copies this book please proof-read it scrupulously against the original, lest the author be accused of errors and true teaching be corrupted.

Danish Invasion

When the Danish king Harold Bluetooth was converted towards the end of the century, his aggressive Christianizing policy sent a fresh wave of heathen vikings seeking liberty at England's expense. Other vikings settled in Normandy. These Normans became Christians, increasingly modelling themselves on the French. But their harbours sheltered heathen vikings.

Olaf Tryggvason of Norway and Harold Bluetooth's son, Swein Forkbeard, led a huge invasion. Bishop Aelfheah of Winchester mediated. He brought Olaf to meet the king at

Andover. A Norse saga says that Olaf had been converted in the Scilly Isles by a hermit, who told a soldier sent to impersonate Olaf, 'You are not the king; but my counsel is that you be true to your king.' At Andover, Bishop Aelfheah confirmed Olaf and he swore to return only in peace.

But the price of peace got higher. Bishop Wulfstan of Worcester later complained that churches were stripped to meet the burden of taxation.

Then Aethelred Evil-Counsel made two momentous decisions. He had a partner who had borne him children, but in 1002 he married Emma, sister of the Duke of Normandy and great-aunt to the future William the Conqueror.

That same year he ordered a massacre of Danes. Many vikings settled in England had embraced Christianity. In Oxford they took refuge in the minster church of St Frideswide. Among them was Swein Forkbeard's sister Gunnhild, who had stayed as hostage. The mob burned the minster down, with the victims inside. The huge Scandinavian population of the Danelaw was outraged. The king of Denmark was now England's sworn enemy.

In 1009 three days of national fasting and prayer were enjoined to counter the viking invasions. Everyone had to go barefoot to church, to make confession. Slaves were freed from work to take part.

In 1011 Canterbury went up in flames. Bishop Aelfheah was now archbishop. Under siege, the abbot of St Augustine's betrayed the city and the Danes broke in. They rounded up a number of ecclesiastics, including Archbishop Aelfheah and the abbess of Minster-in-Thanet, and held them hostage. After looting and burning, they left the cathedral ravaged and went back to their ships, taking the archbishop with them.

They tortured Aelfheah and demanded a ransom. He told them a date by which the money would be forthcoming. But he gave his tenants orders not to pay for his life. When the ransom failed to appear, Aelfheah explained that it was not his fault, merely the result of personal poverty. His incensed captors had the archbishop dragged before them as they feasted at Greenwich. Their leader Thorkell the Tall intervened to defend him, offering anything they asked, except his ship.

But they were too drunk on the captured wine. They pelted the archbishop with meat bones and ox heads. Finally, one of them struck the death-blow to his head with the back of an axe. Aelfheah's body was handed back and buried at St Paul's in London.

In 1013, Northumbria and East Anglia accepted Swein Forkbeard's rule. Oxford, Winchester and London fell to him. King Aethelred and Queen Emma fled to Normandy. Next year, Swein died. The English nobility invited Aethelred Evil-Counsel back, on condition that 'he would govern them more justly than before'.

WULFSTAN OF YORK

King Aethelred lacked good counsel as a young man, but in his later years he had Wulfstan, archbishop of York. Wulfstan was a scholar from the fenlands.

He helped draw up Aethelred Evil-Counsel's later laws. He avoids using the death penalty unnecessarily. The laws condemn heathen practices and the slave trade, especially selling Christians to heathens. In these troubled times there are provisions for a monk who has no monastery and must keep his rule as well as he can. All priests are to be celibate. 'We must all love and honour one God . . . And let us all loyally support our royal lord, and all together defend our lives and our land, as well as ever we can, and pray Almighty God from our inmost heart for his help.'

In 1014 Wulfstan punned on his name to write a rallying 'Sermon of the Wolf to the English'. The Danes are God's judgement upon them. The country is divided and corrupt, with 'wizards and walkyries'. Sponsors and godchildren kill one another. Thanes stand by and watch their womenfolk gang-raped. A crowd lets two or three vikings drive a column of Christians on board their ship to be sold abroad as slaves. Slaves sell their own lords. 'It is the greatest treachery in the world that a man betray his lord's soul; and a full great treachery also that a man betray his lord to death, or drive him in his lifetime from the land.' He is reminding them of Edward the Martyr's murder and Aethelred Evil-Counsel's exile.

Aethelred Evil-Counsel's son Edmund 'Ironside' was defeated by Swein Forkbeard's son Cnut. Bishops and abbots fell among the warriors. Edmund Ironside died a few months later. A whole generation of English princes was dead or in exile. There was no one 'kingworthy' to replace him. Cnut, king of Denmark, became king of England.

Viking invasions had halted building for a while. But even in this time of turmoil and loss, new monasteries were founded, books written, art produced, laity and future monastics educated. Anglo-Saxon excellence in metalwork, jewellery, ivory carving, and embroidery continued. Church music had become more complex. For centuries, Gregorian plainchant had been the English tradition. In the eighth century, embellishments based on popular folk tunes were added. By the tenth century, the singing of two parallel tunes developed into harmony. Instruments were added to the human voice. At St Swithun's in Winchester, the organ had four hundred pipes and needed 70 men to pump it. The boom of its bass notes could be heard across the city.

Denmark was newly Christian. There were not enough Scandinavian clergy to take over the ecclesiastical establishment of England, even if King Cnut had wished. The English Church survived, though spiritually and materially shaken.

The Scandinavian settlement of the north showed itself in stone crosses, decorated in a mixture of English and Scandinavian styles. Cnut was a Christian, but in his army were Danes, Swedes and Norwegians, many of them still proudly heathen. The Christians, too, prized their cultural heritage. Pre-Christian folklore was depicted alongside biblical themes. Favourite characters were the hero Sigurd and the trickster Wayland Smith.

Wulfstan became Cnut's chief counsellor. He had to rethink his condemnation of Danes as the Anti-Christ. Cnut was an enthusiastic Christian. The king paid for promising boys, some from poor homes, to attend monastery schools with a view to ordination. He made a pilgrimage to Rome and protested at the high charges the pope asked English archbishops for their *pallium.* He refounded Bury St Edmunds, lavishing gifts on the shrine of the English king martyred by Danes. But few new monasteries were founded in his reign.

Cnut is remembered as King Canute. One story has him enthroned on the beach, vainly commanding the waves to turn back. It sounds like colossal vainglory. But Cnut's intention was to demonstrate piety in the face of the adulation of his courtiers. How, he asked, could his earthly power compare with that of the Creator King? It was said that afterwards he hung his crown on a crucifix in Winchester and never wore it again.

Under Wulfstan's influence, Cnut's laws forbade the reverence of heathen gods, of sun and moon, stones and trees. Persistent criminals were subject to mutilation, losing hands, feet, eyes, nose, ears, lip or scalp. It sounds savage, but the intention was to avoid taking life. In later centuries, English criminals were hanged for a first offence.

One of Cnut's laws forbids a man to keep another woman besides his wife. But Cnut took Emma of Normandy, widow of Aethelred Evil-Counsel, as his queen, even though he was already married to an ealdorman's daughter.

The *Law of the Northumbrian Priests* probably dates from this time. It grudgingly accepts the continuation of married priests in the north, referring to a clergy wife as the 'priest's woman'. Children are to be baptized within nine days. A priest may not refuse baptism or confession. He is fined for neglecting to shave, for getting drunk and being 'a gleeman or an ale minstrel'. It is forbidden to serve communion wine in a wooden chalice.

BODY-SNATCHING

Cnut raided the tombs of English saints, to enhance the standing of Canterbury, both the cathedral and the abbey. These deeds appear admirable to the churchmen who related them.

In 1023 his target was St Aelfheah, or Alphege, the archbishop vikings pelted to death with ox bones. Londoners treasured his relics at St Paul's. Cnut deployed some of his personal guard to create a disturbance in another part of the city. He posted others on London Bridge and along the Thames, while a third detachment stole the remains. The guards carrying the coffin saw a cloud of dust advancing behind them. They prepared to put up a fight for the saint against the enraged townsfolk. Out of the fog appeared nothing more threatening than the archbishop of Canterbury, following with his own soldiers.

In 1027, Cnut made a pilgrimage to Rome. Caught in a storm on the voyage back, he vowed to St Augustine and St Mildred that he would bring Mildred's relics from Thanet and reinter them at Augustine's abbey. Shipwreck was averted.

Mildred, the early abbess of Minster-in-Thanet, was Kent's best-loved saint. In the ninth century, nuns and townspeople had perished in the flames when the vikings sacked the abbey. Cnut gave the site to St Augustine's, Canterbury. But there was no possibility that the Thanet community would allow their saint's body to be removed. The abbot of St Augustine's joined the Whit Sunday celebrations at Thanet. When everybody else had fallen asleep, he stole into the church, where he was joined by monks and soldiers. All night they wrestled to force the tomb open. They claimed afterwards that Mildred herself came to their aid. Only just in time, they made for their ships. Local people woke and pursued them furiously. King and queen escorted their prize into Canterbury through rejoicing crowds.

It enhanced Cnut's popularity with influential figures in Canterbury. Famous relics enhanced prestige and attracted donations. The importance of physical relics is also evidence of a vivid sense of living in a community linking heaven and earth. Relics of the saints were the live wires of transmission.

EDWARD THE CONFESSOR

Cnut died in 1035. That same year, seven-year-old William, illegitimate son of a tanner's daughter, succeeded his father as Duke of Normandy. He was Queen Emma's great-nephew.

Cnut was succeeded by Harold Harefoot, the son of his uncrowned first wife, and soon after by Harthacnut, his son from Queen Emma. When young Harthacnut dropped dead while chatting to the bride at a wedding reception, it was at last the turn of the son of Emma and her English king, Aethelred Evil-Counsel.

Edward the Confessor was middle-aged and unmarried. He had been exiled to Normandy as a child and had lived abroad ever since. But he was descended from West Saxon kings. The Church welcomed him loyally.

Two years after his coronation, Edward married Edith, daughter of the powerful Earl Godwin of Wessex. Like many of the highest-born women, she had been educated by the nuns of Wilton. She was young, well read and talented, and famous for her needlework.

Edward stripped his mother Emma of her land and possessions, presumably because she had backed her son by Cnut before him. He also deposed her ally, Bishop Stigand of East Anglia. The following year, he rehabilitated both, but Stigand's bishopric had gone to someone else.

Edward introduced friends from many countries into high office. In 1051, Robert of Jumièges became the first Norman archbishop of Canterbury, 15 years ahead of the Norman Conquest. There was not a wholesale replacement of bishops. Edward waited until there was a vacancy, and some of his protégés were English.

In 1051, too, Edward is said to have made his young cousin, Duke William of Normandy, his heir, with his earls' backing.

The Norman archbishop accused the king's father-in-law Earl Godwin of appropriating church land belonging to Canterbury. He hinted at an assassination plot against King Edward. Then a French noble related to Edward caused a massacre of men, women and children in Dover. Earl Godwin demanded his arrest. It ended in rebellion, the queen's father against his sovereign.

Stigand, now bishop of Winchester, attempted reconciliation. In tears, he conveyed King Edward's reply to Earl Godwin. He could have pardon if he would give the king back his brother, who had been fatally blinded by the earl's men years ago in a failed attempt by the princes to gain power in England. Archbishop Robert expelled the earl's supporters, including Spearhavoc, bishop of London. Spearhavoc left, with all the diocesan money he could lay his hands on and the precious materials Edward had given him to make a new crown.

The archbishop advised the king to divorce Edith, Earl Godwin's daughter. Edward resisted, but sent her back to Wilton Abbey. The couple had no child. The story circulated that Edward had never consummated the marriage, to preserve his purity.

Earl Godwin captured the king's fleet in the Thames, with the backing of the people of London. Bishop Stigand negotiated terms. Archbishop Robert and two other Norman bishops fled across the Channel in 'an unseaworthy ship'. Edith and her family were restored to court. King Edward kept many Normans, but Archbishop Robert was not recalled to Canterbury.

The primacy went to Stigand of Winchester. It was against church law for a bishop to take a see whose rightful incumbent was still alive. Rome judged the expulsion of Robert illegal. The pope excommunicated Stigand. He continued to hold the job. Robert's death failed to resolve the dispute. It was a significant factor in the papal blessing of William of Normandy's invasion of England.

The bond between king and Church, dazzlingly symbolized in Edward's coronation, was beginning to be questioned. The king's favourite bishops each held several dioceses. There was a suspicion that ecclesiastical offices were changing hands for payment. Those suspected of simony ranged from the king to local landowners. In a culture which practised gift-giving on a huge scale, the charges could not be proved.

Eleventh-century bishops were lawmakers, ambassadors, army commanders, judges. Literate clergy administered the secular state. Edward paid them well. But others questioned whether this was the Church's job.

HAROLD AND WILLIAM

In 1055 the Welsh attacked Hereford. The cathedral clergy stationed themselves at the door of their new minster to prevent looting. They were killed where they stood. The Welsh burned the cathedral. They sacked the city and surrounding countryside, taking away strings of captives to be sold as slaves. The bishop of Hereford died soon afterwards. Edward sent the queen's brother, Earl Harold Godwinsson, to exact vengeance. But he felt Harold was not tough enough and appointed a very different bishop of Hereford. Leofgar was a warrior bishop. He shocked people by wearing a moustache after he was priested. He led a force against the Welsh prince but was defeated and killed.

Around 1064, Harold Godwinsson went to Normandy. The Bayeux Tapestry shows him swearing loyalty to Duke William and giving him a ring and sword, as pledge of Edward's intention that he should be the next king of England.

Edward was still childless. His great project was the restoration of an old abbey on an island in the Thames. To build and endow this, he diverted revenue from abbeys across the country. Its crowning glory was its new church, Westminster, planned as Edward's burial place. It was large, with a central tower, and of a plain beauty, in the English manner. By the end of 1065, Edward was too ill to attend its consecration. He died in the new year. His shrouded body was carried through the streets on an open bier, attended by singing clergy and choristers with bells. He was buried at Westminster.

Edward was praised as 'the Confessor' for his supposedly celibate life. He was not noticeably religious until late in life. His real passion was hunting. He contributed little to the good of his people.

Harold Godwinsson claimed that Edward had made him his heir on his deathbed, in the presence of his sister the queen and the archbishop of Canterbury. Edward had roused from his coma, uttering a dire prophecy about the fate of England under leaders, religious and secular, in the devil's service. Archbishop Stigand dismissed this as delirium and senility.

Harold Godwinsson convinced the witan. On the very day of Edward the Confessor's funeral and in the same church of Westminster, he was crowned king of England.

William of Normandy accused Harold of breaking his oath. Harold replied that the oath was worthless, because he had not had the consent of the people of England. It was like the oath of a maiden living under her father's roof, which the law held invalid if made without her parents' knowledge. William appealed to the pope. The pope sent a standard in token of his blessing.

In 1066, two enemies fell on England in quick succession. In September, King Harold Godwinsson defeated a force led by Harald the Ruthless of Norway and his own brother at Stamford Bridge. Only 24 ships were needed to carry away the survivors from 300. The success lasted four days. When Duke William came ashore at Pevensey, Harold had a smaller force to oppose him. At 'the ancient apple tree' at Hastings, he was shot through the eye by an arrow. It was the close of an era for England and the English Church.

William the Conqueror was consecrated king of England on Christmas Day 1066, in Edward's new church at Westminster. He was led to the altar steps by both English archbishops. Before the crown was given to him, the people were asked, in French and English, whether they would have William as their king. The guards outside mistook the shout of acclaim for an attack on their lord and set fire to the buildings around them. William was anointed and crowned by Ealdred of York, not Stigand of Canterbury. Stigand's legitimacy, like the future of the English Church, was in doubt.

12
Under New Management

REBELLION

Pope Alexander had sent William a standard to symbolize his blessing of the invasion. William sent the pope Harold's captured banner. The English kingdom and the English Church were now subject to William. The pope may not have intended wholesale conquest.

William appointed his half-brother Odo, bishop of Bayeux, as the new earl of Kent. Odo commissioned the Bayeux Tapestry, showing the lead-up to William's succession. The design tells the Norman point of view, although it was embroidered in England. In 1067 William returned to Normandy, leaving Odo in charge. He proved a harsh ruler. There were rebellions all over England, with the bitterest fighting in the north. Bishops played an active part. William returned in anger and devastated the rebellious areas, particularly northern England.

The abbey of Peterborough found itself caught between a rock and a hard place. William had appointed a Norman, Turold, with a reputation as a hard man, to take over the abbacy. Hearing of this, the English rebel Hereward the Wake decided to loot it before the Normans got there. The monks got wind of this. The sacristan, whose responsibility the church furnishings were, grabbed everything he could: Gospels, vestments, small items of gold and silver. He fled to Turold, asked protection and revealed the outlaws' plans. Hereward's band came by ship over the fens, but the monks barricaded themselves in the monastery. The rebels set fire to it and the monks emerged to beg for peace. The outlaws broke into the church and climbed the great cross to seize Christ's golden crown and the stool of red gold under his feet. They found the precious altar-frontal hidden up in the tower, took two gold shrines and nine silver ones, and 15 large gold and silver crosses. They said they were acting out of loyalty to the monastery. When Turold reached Peterborough, he found only one monk, too sick to leave his bed. The rest crept back a week later. The outlaws took the stolen artefacts to Ely and delivered them to the Danes. The treasures of Peterborough were scattered across Scandinavia.

New Bishops

William's decision to appoint his own men as bishops was political, rather than religious. Bishops had been influential in the uprisings. What Edward the Confessor had started to do piecemeal, William set about wholesale. He called for a papal legation to purge the Church for him and also to legitimize his own position.

By the time of the conquest, only one English bishop was married. Before the decisive council of Winchester could meet in 1070, this bishop resigned his see, realizing that the day of his kind was over. The Winchester council deposed Archbishop Stigand and other bishops whom William suspected of backing the English revolt. Soon, even English bishops not suspected of sedition were out. William's bishops were deputy military commanders as well as ecclesiastical princes.

William had a monastery built at the site of the battle. Under the papal legates' scrutiny, the new Norman bishops drew up a list of penances for crimes committed by their army during the heat of warfare. William wanted to start with a clean sheet. He had himself crowned again by the papal legates. He may still have been uneasy about the involvement of Stigand in his first anointing.

Lanfranc

William's choice for Canterbury was Lanfranc. He was a lawyer's son from Pavia, in Lombardy, but preferred a career in language and rhetoric. It was a culture shock to arrive in Normandy and find he needed to be a priest to follow an intellectual profession. He taught at the cathedral school at Avranches until he was set upon by thieves in the woods and vowed that, if he escaped with his life, he would become a monk. At the austere monastery of Bec, monks laboured in the fields on a diet of black bread and vegetables. Lanfranc turned it into a leading teaching abbey.

Lanfranc's career break came in 1053, when William, Duke of Normandy, married Mathilda, daughter of the count of Flanders. The pope had forbidden the match, on the grounds that the pair were closely related. The story is that William sent his chaplain to Lanfranc to ask his help in defending the marriage. Lanfranc found the chaplain's arguments so hilarious that he presented him with an ABC. William ordered Lanfranc out of Normandy, and trashed Bec's abbey farm. As Lanfranc was riding away from Bec, he fell in with William. 'Can't you get away quicker than that?' asked the duke. 'I could if I had a decent horse,' retorted Lanfranc. William laughed, paid the abbey compensation and made Lanfranc his adviser on church affairs. Lanfranc persuaded Rome to recognize the marriage and was made abbot of Caen.

In 1070, William sent for him to take over Canterbury. Lanfranc's objections sound like those of Augustine's monks. He is an Italian and does not speak the English language. He has no idea how to handle barbarians. William was no more sympathetic than Pope Gregory.

It was not an encouraging start. In 1067, Canterbury's cathedral was gutted by fire. Historic archives were lost and the title deeds of Christ Church's huge estates were reduced to ashes. Worse, in the common people's eyes, the shrines of beloved English saints were destroyed. Lanfranc's consecration took place in a temporary wooden structure within the ruins.

CANTERBURY VERSUS YORK

He immediately ran into trouble with York. Thomas of Bayeux had been given the archbishopric, but had yet to be consecrated. Lanfranc asked for a written declaration of York's obedience to Canterbury. No archbishop of York had ever made such a promise. Thomas refused and left without consecration.

The king backed Lanfranc. Thomas gave in, with the promise that the position of his successors would be reviewed. While they were both in Rome receiving their *palliums*, Thomas raised the matter with the pope. He wanted to achieve Gregory's vision, the primacy alternating between Canterbury and York. Lanfranc scored a low blow. He pointed out that Thomas was the son of a priest. Rome's views on celibacy meant that he should not have been eligible for the priesthood.

At the council at Winchester in 1072 Lanfranc rehearsed the historical evidence for Canterbury's primacy. He avoided the question of why York needed to promise obedience, and Thomas failed to raise it. The boundary between the provinces moved north to the Humber. England had 15 sees. Lanfranc took 13. Thomas was left the huge dioceses of York and Durham. He was also given responsibility for Scotland. The Scottish bishops took no notice of this. Nor did the Welsh accept Canterbury's authority. The clergy of St David's asserted that their foundation was far older.

William supported Lanfranc. An independent archbishopric was politically dangerous, particularly in the north. There was the possibility of a breakaway province, whose archbishop might crown a rival king. The papacy, however, saw Canterbury's claim as a challenge to its authority. It was not in Rome's interest to have one archbishop so powerful he could command another. In 1123, York was declared independent of Canterbury, though acknowledging its primacy.

Change in the Church

Lanfranc set about reform. The Normans viewed the English Church as ignorant and corrupt. The English nobility were said to be slipshod in their religious observance, having morning prayers gabbled in their bedchambers by a chaplain, while they dallied with their wives, instead of getting up and going to church. When they got their female servants pregnant, they sold them as prostitutes or foreign slaves.

Lanfranc moved rural bishops' seats into towns. Alfred's siting of minsters in burghs had gone some way towards urbanizing

146

the Church. Before the Conquest, the bishop of Chester-le-Street had moved to Durham for greater safety, taking Cuthbert's body, and the bishop of Crediton had moved to Exeter. But the English had no love of cities. Early rural abbeys had left sees based in small country towns, even villages. Now, Sherborne was transferred to Salisbury, Selsey to Chichester, Lichfield to Chester, and soon Dorchester-on-Thames to Lincoln, Elmham to Norwich, and Wells to Bath.

The Church became more hierarchical. Only bishops and abbots could speak at synods. Parish priests lost this right. Dioceses were divided into archdeaconries, and eventually subdivided into rural deaneries. The village priests remained English, but there was a culture clash with their new Norman landowners. Parish priests in England had enjoyed more security and freedom than in continental Europe. Norman nobles were accustomed to having their own way.

Lanfranc reinforced laws against clergy marriage. Married canons must separate from their wives immediately, though parish clergy might remain with their families. All future deacons and priests were to take a vow of celibacy. In practice, though, the old English custom of married clergy took a long time to disappear.

ABBEYS

Abbeys were of less importance. Abbots who had supported the rebellion went immediately. Other English abbots were replaced as the opportunity presented itself. Lanfranc drew up a constitution for Canterbury's monks, based on the most recent form of the Benedictine Rule. It laid down regulations for every detail of monastery life. Monks and nuns at any house using it would know exactly what they should be doing, when and where.

Lanfranc would have liked to remove all the monastic cathedral chapters and replace them with secular canons, reversing Dunstan's policy. The process was gradual, but the number of monk-bishops dwindled.

Lanfranc was kind to his own monks. The English Eadmer tells how he gave money to those with poor families. One, probably Eadmer himself, received five shillings every other month for his mother. On one visit she did not notice the money wrapped in cloth. When she mentioned the lack of it next time Eadmer realized it was lost. He was afraid to tell Lanfranc, but the bishop noticed his disconsolate face and called him aside. When Eadmer told him, he said, 'Don't look so mournful. God must have seen that somebody else needed it more. Here's seven shillings for your five. But don't tell the others.'

There was a revival of asceticism. The English abbot of Evesham had opened his gates to refugees fleeing the persecution of the north. He sent three monks back to the north-east, where they found the once glorious Wearmouth and Jarrow in desolate ruins. They rebuilt a local community. In 1083, the Norman bishop of Durham's cathedral invited them to move there. They founded a priory with a lifestyle reminiscent of the hermit Cuthbert. It was the forerunner of a coming challenge to moderate Benedictinism.

RESISTANCE

Resentment flared again in the north. Bishop Walker of Durham came from Lorraine. He ruled his new diocese like a prince and appointed two relatives to administer public and church business. The bishop turned a blind eye to their excesses, until the pair caused the death of one of his English servants. This man had a local reputation for his sanctity and devotion to St Cuthbert. The terrified bishop realized the implications and offered the family legal redress. But the Northumbrians were bent on revenge. As one of the guilty pair left the church after the hearing, the mob lynched him. Outside the gates, Bishop Walker tried to remonstrate with them. He was killed too. The other conspirator barricaded himself inside the church. The mob set fire to it and he was forced out, in flames, to die on a host of spears.

There was trouble at Glastonbury. In 1083, the Norman abbot Thurstin tried to introduce a new French chant, to replace the old English Gregorian tradition. When the monks argued, the abbot threatened them. It came to blows. The abbot called for military reinforcements and the monks fled into the church for sanctuary. Soldiers rushing in after them found the monks pleading at the altar for God's mercy. The troop took up positions in the gallery and fired arrows down into the sanctuary, until they bristled from the crucifix. Some monks crawled under the altar. Three were killed and 18 wounded. The rest fled. William realized the abbot had gone too far. Thurstin was exiled.

ENGLISH SAINTS

Sainthood, in the Anglo-Saxon Church, was a matter of public acclaim. People knew the great Christians they had loved in life, or who had witnessed to Christ through a martyr's death. They made pilgrimages to their heroes' tombs, miracles were reported and cults began. Relics played a large part in Anglo-Saxon spirituality. The Lady of the Mercians' patriotic dedications to Oswald and Alkmund meant nothing to the newcomers.

Lanfranc found the relics of great English saints under the charred remains of Christ Church, Canterbury. There was Dunstan, Aelfheah who had been killed with ox bones, Wilfrid, whose remains had been transferred from Ripon, and many more. He reinterred them with dignity in the western apse of the new cathedral. But elsewhere it was a different story. At Malmesbury, Aldhelm's relics were preserved, but the rest thrown out as rubbish. The bones of King Offa of Mercia were ejected from St Albans. Many English saints were removed from the church calendar.

It was not a blanket ban. The disinterments had an interesting effect. Questions were asked. Who were these people? What had they done? Did they deserve to be called saints? It led to new English saints' *Lives* being written, some by Normans.

Lanfranc set little store by miracles and superstition. Traditionally, a procession brought relics to be enshrined at the altar of a new church. At the consecration of Lanfranc's new cathedral on Palm Sunday, 1077, the procession through the streets of Canterbury carried instead the bread and wine of Christ's body and blood.

English men and women had enriched their churches with their excellence in illumination, precious metalwork and embroidery. The Norman enthusiasm was for big buildings. They pulled down Anglo-Saxon churches, often quite recently built, and replaced them with more massive ones. The cathedrals they raised in England were bigger than those in Normandy. Unfortunately, they were not yet skilled enough to prevent some of the central towers collapsing. The informal clusters of English monastery buildings were swept away. A centralized design, every part connected to the whole, asserted new authority.

WULFSTAN OF WORCESTER

Wulfstan of Worcester, last of the English bishops, worked well with Lanfranc and was a zealous campaigner for celibacy in his clergy. He began his career in King Edward's reign as a monk. But he cared for the crowds outside the monastery gates. He spent hours preaching to them and ministering to their needs. Wulfstan was attacked by fellow monks for involvement with the outside world. He retorted, 'Bothered by people? That's what I'm here for.' As bishop of Worcester, he travelled ceaselessly around his diocese. His summer confirmation services would last a whole day.

Wulfstan had a refreshing interpretation of his role as spiritual adviser to the rich. He got so tired of one noblewoman, wasting his time with her outpourings of religiosity, that he boxed her ears.

The story of his confrontation with Lanfranc at the council of Westminster may be exaggerated, but it rings true in spirit. Wulfstan was one of those accused of sedition after the uprising against the Normans. The proceedings were in French, which he did not speak. He was given time to prepare his defence but, to the dismay of his supporters, spent it in saying the canonical office due at that hour. Lanfranc ordered him to hand over his episcopal ring and staff. Through his interpreter, Wulfstan retorted that he had never thought himself worthy to bear them, but since they had been given to him by King Edward, he would return them to him only. He stuck his staff between the stones of Edward's tomb, took off his ring and sat down. No Norman, it was said, could remove the staff. Lanfranc confirmed Wulfstan in his post.

Wulfstan proved loyal to William and Lanfranc, but his social conscience continued unabated. He visited the port of Bristol, which even then was a slave port, and attacked the slave trade. He pleaded with the dealers and preached against their harsh treatment of slaves. He got Lanfranc on his side. They persuaded the king to withdraw his approval, though it meant a loss of royal revenue. Slavery decreased under William.

EDUCATION

With the new cathedral at Canterbury complete, Lanfranc planned his bishop's palace. Like Aethelwold of Winchester, Lanfranc created an ecclesiastical city within the secular one. He demolished 27 houses to clear the site, then surrounded cathedral, palace and monastery with an inner wall.

Outside the city, he built a leper hospital, an old people's home and a new church, dedicated to St Gregory. The canons of St Gregory conducted services for local people free of charge and ran a town grammar school. Lanfranc revived the cathedral school at Christ Church by bringing in a gifted French monk. But his intention there was to improve the education of monks, not lay students. Education was shifting away from the monasteries. Secular schools started to appear in the London area, part of a wider European movement. The duty of monks and nuns was to be stable, obedient, anonymous, concerned above all with communal worship. Individual initiative and outreach were not expected of them.

WILLIAM AND THE PAPACY

In the time of Edgar, Church and State reached their highest point of oneness. William had other plans. Ecclesiastical business was separated from the secular courts. William was not going to have his actions governed by the Church. William had sought papal blessing for his invasion in 1066. But he would not swear an oath of loyalty to the see of Rome. There had recently been two popes competing for legitimacy. In future, England would not recognize any pope, nor receive papal letters, without the king's permission. Papal legates must address themselves to the king and not assume authority over the Church in England. Bishops must obtain his leave before visiting Rome. None of his barons could be excommunicated without William's consent.

Lanfranc supported him. The archbishop was, not surprisingly, summoned urgently to Rome, with a threat to remove his spiritual authority. There is no record that he went. But his agenda was different from William's. The papacy gave him a useful canopy of authority. He collected all the canons of doctrine approved by the Catholic Church through the centuries and deposited a copy in Canterbury Cathedral. The English Church could no longer pick and choose.

English monarchs had always had power over the choice of bishops. It was traditionally the king who gave the bishop his ring and staff, even led him to his throne. But now William was demanding that the English Church assert an independence from the papacy greater than any other country. It was a far cry from Boniface's loyalty. It resembled, in one way, the early position of the Anglo-Celtic Church, acknowledging the primacy of the Bishop of Rome, but not his absolute authority. Yet William was also challenging both Celtic and Roman understanding of the balance of power between English Church and king. William was to be God's viceregent in England.

He made all the English swear loyalty directly to him, above their lords.

William was seated at a feast, resplendent in jewelled crown and royal robes. A jester cried out, 'Behold, I see God!' The king ordered him to be whipped. As fools do, he had come dangerously close to the truth.

The Lord's Companions

Loyalty was the fundamental question for Anglo-Saxon Christians. To the old gods or Christ? To Rome or Iona? To the vision of the hermit Cuthbert or the princely Wilfrid? To a national Church or a larger realm?

The Anglo-Saxon Church sprang from minsters, monasteries and hermit missionaries. It was continually inspired by Christian communities. Their spiritual success brought wealth and power, and with it, temptation. The movement continually needed to reinvent itself. We rarely hear the voices of the parish priests, the laity. The monastic witness is partial, but evidence, too, of the commitment and achievement of these loyal bands of companions.

The glory of the Anglo-Saxon Church lies not in its original scholarship but in its gifted teachers. Hild, Aldhelm, Leoba, Alcuin, were remembered with admiration and affection by their pupils for the rest of their lives. Like loyal lords, they sustained their followers with a lasting bond.

If England were to choose a new patron saint, it should perhaps be a layman. Alfred the Great showed that it was possible, within the terms of his violent times, to live the Christian life to the full. Hours devoted to prayer led directly to creative action. The cities he built were spiritual as well as defensive. He wanted professional Christians to share the gifts of the Spirit with the laity. He negotiated a peace between hostile communities based on mutual respect.

In an age that has lost its faith in communities and grown cynical about leaders, their story challenges us. The highest value of the Anglo-Saxons was loyalty, not to kin or to kingdom, but to a personal lord. When they carved 'The Dream of the Rood' in runes on the Ruthwell Cross, they were pledging their lives as companions to their hero Christ, who gave his life for them.

Further Reading

There is a wealth of early source material in translation and recent commentary on this period. Here is a selection.

Aldhelm, *Aldhelm: The Prose Works*, tr. Lapidge, M. and Herren, M., D. S. Brewer, Ipswich and Rowman and Littlefield, NJ 1979.

Alexander, M. (ed. and tr.), *The Earliest English Poems*. Penguin 1991.

Backhouse, J., *The Lindisfarne Gospels*. Phaidon 1987.

Barlow, F., *The English Church 1000–1066*. Longman 1963.

Barlow, F., *Edward the Confessor*. Eyre Methuen 1979.

Barlow, F., *The English Church 1066–1154*. Longman 1979.

Barlow, F., *The Norman Conquest and Beyond*. Hambledon 1983.

Bede, *A History of the English Church and People*, ed. and tr. Shirley-Price, L., rev. Latham, R. E. Penguin 1968.

Blair, P. H., *An Introduction to Anglo-Saxon England*. Cambridge University Press 1966.

Branston, B., *The Lost Gods of England*. Constable 1957.

Brooks, N. and Cubitt, C. (eds), *St Oswald of Worcester*. Leicester University Press 1996.

Campbell, J., John, E. and Wormald, P. (eds), *The Anglo-Saxons*. Penguin 1982.

Colgrave, B. (ed. and tr.), *Two Lives of Saint Cuthbert: A Life by an Anonymous Monk of Lindisfarne and Bede's Prose Life*. Cambridge University Press 1956.

Douglas, D. C. and Greenaway, G. W. (eds), *English Historical Documents 1042–1189*. Eyre and Spottiswoode 1953.

Duckett, E. S., *Alcuin, Friend of Charlemagne: His World and His Work*. Macmillan 1951.

Duckett, E. S., *Saint Dunstan of Canterbury: A Study of Monastic Reform in the Tenth Century*. Collins 1955.

Duckett, E. S., *Anglo-Saxon Saints and Scholars*. Archon 1967.

Farmer, D. H. (ed.), *The Age of Bede: Bede: Life of Cuthbert, Eddius Stephanus: Life of Wilfrid, Bede: Lives of the Abbots of Wearmouth and Jarrow, with The Voyage of St Brendan*, tr. Webb, J. F. and Farmer, D. H. Penguin 1983.

Felix, *Felix's Life of Saint Guthlac*, ed. and tr. Colgrave, B. Cambridge University Press 1956.

Gibson, M., *Lanfranc of Bec.* Clarendon 1978.

Gildas, *The Ruin of Britain and Other Works*, ed. and tr. Winterbottom, M. Phillimore 1978.

Giles, J. A. (ed.), *William of Malmesbury's Chronicle of the Kings of England from the Earliest Period to the Reign of King Stephen.* Bohn 1847.

Godfrey, J., *The Church in Anglo-Saxon England.* Cambridge University Press 1962.

Harton, S., *Stars Appearing: Lives of Sixty-Eight Saints of the Anglican Calendar.* Hodder & Stoughton 1954.

Jones, C. W., *Saints' Lives and Chronicles in Early England: Together with the First English Translations of The Oldest Life of Pope St Gregory the Great by a Monk of Whitby and The Life of St Guthlac of Crowland by Felix.* Cornell University Press 1947.

Keynes, S. and Lapidge, M. (eds and trs), *Alfred the Great: Asser's Life of King Alfred and other contemporary sources.* Penguin 1983.

Lawson, M. K., *Cnut: The Danes in England in the Early Eleventh Century.* Longman 1993.

Marsden, J., *Northanhymbre Saga: The History of the Anglo-Saxon Kings of Northumbria.* Kyle Cathie 1992.

Mayr-Harting, H., *The Coming of Christianity to Anglo-Saxon England.* Batsford 1972.

Sampson, F., *Visions and Voyages: The Story of our Celtic Heritage.* Triangle, SPCK 1998.

Savage, A. (ed. and tr.), *The Anglo-Saxon Chronicles.* Phoebe Phillips/Heinemann 1982.

Scott, D., *An Anglo-Saxon Passion.* SPCK 1999.

Stansbury, D., *The Lady Who Fought the Vikings.* Imogen 1993.

Stenton, F. M., *Anglo-Saxon England.* Oxford University Press 1989.

Talbot, C. H. (ed.), *The Anglo-Saxon Missionaries in Germany: Being the Lives of SS Willibrord, Boniface, Sturm, Leoba and Lebuin, together with the Hoeoeporicon of St Willibald and a selection from the correspondence of St Boniface.* Sheed and Ward 1954.

Whitelock, D., *The Beginnings of English Society.* Penguin 1972.

Whitelock, D. (ed.), *English Historical Documents c. 500–1042.* Eyre Methuen, London and Oxford University Press, NY 1979.

Index and Glossary

Gosforth, Map of Britain, 10

Gospel books 49, 51, 67, 87–8, 100, 143

Greek 64–5, 77, 103

Greenwich, Map of Britain, 134

Gregory, the Great, Pope, 6–7th C viii, 21–6, 28, 34–6, 65, 68, 72, 81–2, 84–5, 104, 112, 145–6, 151 Gregorian chant 36, 136, 148

Gregory II, Pope, 8th C 93

Grim, Woden disguised 9 Grimes Graves, Norfolk flint mines 9 Grimsdykes, earthworks 9

Grimbald, 9th C Flemish scholar 111

Gunnhild, 11th C Danish princess 134

Guthlac, 7–8th C hermit of Crowland ix, 82–5, 96

Guthrum, 9th C Danish king of East Anglia 110

Gwynedd, British kingdom, Map of Britain, 36

Hadrian, 7th C African abbot of Canterbury 64–5, 77

Hadrian, Pope, 8th C 102–3

Hadrian's Wall, Map of Britain, 5, 14, 16, 25, 38

Harald the Ruthless, 11th C king of Norway 142

Harold Bluetooth, 10th C king of Denmark and Norway 133

Harold Godwinsson, 11th C king of England x, 141–3

Harold Harefoot, 11th C king of England 138

Harrow-on-the-Hill, Map of Britain, 26

Harthacnut, 11th C king of Denmark and England 138

Hartlepool, Map of Britain, viii, 46, 56, 106

Harz Mountains, Map of Europe, 92

Hastings, Map of Britain, 18, 142

Hatfield Chase, Map of Britain, 36

Heavenfield, Map of Britain, 38

heathenism, reversion to 29–33, 35–8, 40, 43–4, 54, 63, 90–2, 110, 133

Hebrides, Map of Britain, 70

Heidenheim, Map of Europe, 97

Heiu, 7th C abbess of Hartlepool 46, 57

Helena, 3rd–4th C Roman empress 86

Heligoland, Map of Europe, 91

Hengest, 5th C leader of Jutish mercenaries viii, 15–16

Hereford, Map of Britain, 140–1

Hereric, 6–7th C Deiran prince 28, 31

Hereswith, 7th C Northumbrian princess 32, 45

Hereward the Wake, 11th C rebel leader 143–4

hermit, seeking God in solitude 27, 39, 41–2, 57–8, 65, 69, 71–2, 81–4, 87, 110, 120, 134, 153

Hertford, synod of, Map of Britain, ix, 65

Hesse, Map of Europe, 93, 95

Hewald the Black, 8th C missionary to Saxony 91

Hewald the White, 8th C missionary to Saxony 91

Hexham, Map of Britain, ix, 38, 66–9, 73, 88

hide, area needed to support one family 56, 59

Hild, 7th C abbess of Whitby viii–ix, 28, 32, 34, 45–6, 56–7, 59–60, 67, 70, 75, 80, 108, 153

Hippo, on North African coast 113

History of the English Church and People 37, 39, 81–2

Hnaef, 5th C Danish king 15

Hoder, Norse god 12

Holstein, Map of Europe, 4

Honorius, 7th C archbishop of Canterbury 31, 34, 57

Honorius, Pope, 7th C 35, 42

Horsa, 5th C Anglo-Saxon mercenary leader 15

Housesteads, Roman fort, Map of Britain, 14

Hretha, Anglo-Saxon goddess 10

Humber, River, Map of Britain, 4, 18, 22, 27, 29, 34, 36, 53, 65, 90, 100, 146

Huneberc, 7th C Heidenheim nun 97

Hungary, Map of Europe, 103

Icanhoe, unknown site in East Anglia 80

Icel, 6th C king of Norfolk 19

Ida, 6th C king of Bernicia 18

Idle, River, Map of Britain, 29

India 4

Indo-European 4

Ine, 7–8th C king of Wessex 72–3, 78, 118

Ingeld, Anglo-Saxon hero 105

Inishboffin, Map of Europe, 62

Iona, Map of Britain, viii, 20, 30, 37–9, 44–6, 48, 59–63, 70, 153

Ipswich, Map of Britain, 19

Ireland, Map of Europe, 4, 14, 42, 45, 50, 55–6, 62–3, 77, 90, 106–7, 109, 114, 116 Irish viii, 1, 5, 14–16, 47, 70, 116 Irish Church 20–2, 38, 41, 45, 50, 54–60, 62, 76–8, 85, 93–5, 118, 121

Irene, 9th C Roman empress 103

Isidore, 6–7th C Spanish scholar 82